Understanding JESUS

Understanding JESUS

Cultural Insights into the Words and Deeds of Christ

JOE AMARAL

New York Boston Nashville

FaithWords
Hachette Book Group
237 Park Avenue
New York, NY 10017

www.faithwords.com

Printed in the United States of America

First Edition: April 2011

10 9 8 7 6 5 4 3 2 1

Library of Congress Cataloging-in-Publication Data
Amaral, Joe.
Understanding Jesus : cultural insights into the words and deeds of Christ / by Joe Amaral. — 1st ed.
p. cm.
ISBN 978-0-446-58476-0
1. Jesus Christ—Jewishness. I. Title.
BT590.J8A43 2011
232.9'01—dc22

2010044429

This book is dedicated in loving memory to my father, Francisco Amaral. His faith, passion, and love for God and his family have deeply impacted me and will remain with me all my life. I look forward to the day when we will meet again.

Francisco Amaral
September 22, 1946–October 22, 2008

Acknowledgments

I wish to thank my precious wife, Karen, for her faithful support and for the countless hours she spent typing, editing, and formatting this book. She has always been my greatest fan. When I felt like giving up and when it seemed like I would never finish writing this book, she always had the right words at the right time. God knew what He was doing when He brought her into my life.

I want to thank both our children, Katelyn and Daniel, for being so understanding with Daddy's travel schedule. They say they're proud of me, but it's me who is proud of them.

I want to thank my mom for always praying and for always believing in me. My parents worked so hard and gave up so much not only for me but for all their family.

Also, I want to express deep gratitude to my inlaws, Clyde and Marion Williamson, who have loved me like their own son. They have contributed in so many ways to this project. Their prayers and support have never wavered.

The writing of this book would not have been possible without the editing skills of James D. Craig. He motivated me, he challenged me, and he made me better. I'm so thankful for his commitment to excellence and for the days and hours he poured into this project.

Contents

Understanding
JESUS

Introduction

A Remarkable Discovery

Have you ever wondered who Jesus really was? I mean really wondered who He was as a person who lived and walked on this earth? It's a pretty wild topic when you stop and think about it. Here is the Son of the Living God—alive and dwelling with man. What a thought!

Then comes the question of what was He like? What kinds of things did He do or say? What kind of a person was He? In order to answer some of those questions I believe we have to reprocess the information we have come to accept about Him.

In November of 2002, I had the opportunity to visit the land of Israel for a couple of weeks. One day we were standing on one of the most famous historic spots.

From where we stood you can look down upon a breathtaking view of Jerusalem. It was from this place, or one like it, the Scriptures tell us in Matthew 9:36, that Jesus was moved with compassion for the people of Jerusalem. As you look to the right you can see the ancient Jewish burial sites and the tombs of some of Israel's greatest kings and Old Testament legends. In the center, your eyes fall upon the Old City of David and the Kidron Valley, where Jesus and His disciples walked numerous times. To the far and upper right you can see the Mount of Olives, where Jesus will set foot when He returns, and you can see where the Temple used to stand. To the upper left you see the splendor of the Old City of Jerusalem with its massive walls. What a breathtaking sight! As I stood there, I felt as though I could have lived in that moment forever.

Then I turned to a friend who was near me and told him that I had just made a remarkable discovery. By the look on my face and the size of my eyes he knew that whatever it was, it was big. No doubt he was wondering what incredible thought or unbelievable revelation I had received that would change our lives and our world. I said to him, "Jesus was a Jew!" As soon as I said it, I grabbed my mouth and covered it. I couldn't believe what I had just said. He gave me a look of mock bewilderment and said, "You mean He wasn't from Montana?"

Only moments later did I realize the full impact that statement had on me. Jesus wasn't from Montana, nor was He a Canadian—He was a Jew living in first-century Israel, living a first-century lifestyle.

That realization has forever impacted the way I see Jesus and the way in which I now perceive the Gospels. During the rest of the trip, as I looked around me at the people, the land and buildings, the importance of this simple statement became more and more powerful. This is where Jesus lived and died, where He rose from the dead, and it is the land and people to which He will return.

Out of that realization also came a deep desire from within my spirit—I would make it my purpose in life to discover the historic Jesus Who lived and taught in the land of Israel. What were people like in the time of Jesus? What were their thoughts? What was going on in the world around them? How did it affect Israel? And what kind of Messiah were they expecting?

As I began to ask the questions I also began to seek out some answers. I read books, I researched on the Internet, I sat under the teaching of rabbis and Messianic Jewish believers, and I pleaded with them to tell me Who Jesus really was. The pages that follow are the product of my ongoing quest to find the answers to these and other, similar questions.

As you read this book I pray that the Spirit of Messiah will captivate you as He has me. May the God of all wisdom and peace favor you this day.

First-Century Idioms

To understand the sayings of Jesus as they were originally intended, it is important to lay a foundation for our thought process. Idioms essentially are words or phrases that belong to a particular language, group of people, geographical region, or period of history.

In order to better understand what is meant by the term "idiom" it will help to think in terms of some common English idioms used in American English. Every day we use phrases such as "straight from the horse's mouth" or "it's raining cats and dogs." Statements like these make no sense when interpreted literally; however, for many Americans they need no explanation. Anyone living in the United States would instantly understand the message of such idioms.

Let's take this thought one step further. Imagine going to a land in the Middle East or into the depths of the African jungle and using these idioms in attempting to communicate with those from that land. What would people in a remote part of Africa think if, in the middle of a rainstorm, you were to tell them that it was "raining cats and dogs"? Could you imagine the expression on their faces? Could you see them running outside to see if cats and dogs were actually falling down on them from the heavens? What if their spiritual leaders attempted to assimilate that saying into their culture without fully understanding its intended meaning?

This may sound like a ridiculous example, but are

we not guilty of doing the very same thing in terms of how we understand the New Testament? We have taken the sayings of Jesus and used them simplistically in developing our doctrines and theology while failing to understand the true meaning of many of the idioms used by Christ. As we strive to be more like our Messiah, to think and act like Him, then understanding what He actually meant must be our greatest priority.

As we embrace the rich Jewish heritage of Jesus we can then begin to understand His teachings and actions more accurately. For example, why didn't Jesus ever come right out and say that He was the Messiah? Are you sure He didn't? If we can learn something of how His contemporaries understood what He said and did, we will discover that Jesus did in fact claim to be the Christ, the Messiah of Israel. He used something called the hinting method (also known in Hebrew as the Remez method) when He taught. This method of teaching was commonly used in the first century by rabbis when making a point in their debates over the meaning of the Torah or the Old Testament law. A rabbi would quote a verse in part and that would immediately draw the minds of the audience to the entire portion of Scripture he was referring to. The intended meaning was not only the actual words quoted but the entire passage where they were recorded.

Another method would be to answer a question with a question. For example, when the teachers of the law questioned Jesus about whether or not to pay taxes to Caesar, He answered their question with another question: "Whose image is on the coin?" This and countless more truths await you as you discover who Yeshua (Jesus) really was.

The Life of Jesus

This book is organized around the life of Jesus on a loosely chronological basis. Teaching on a variety of passages is covered in sequence as each incident occurs. While scholars do not agree on the sequence of every detail mentioned in the Gospels, there is a significant consensus surrounding most of the events in Christ's life. The Gospels do not provide us with a detailed *chronological* picture of His life because they were not intended to be mere biographies of a great man. The four Evangelists were telling the story first and foremost in order to proclaim the Good News that God's Son, the Messiah of Israel, had come to reconcile men and women to God through His life, death, and resurrection. Each one selected and arranged the material at his disposal in order to paint a particular portrait of Christ aimed at a specific audience. It is believed that Matthew wrote for a Jewish audience, Mark for the Romans, Luke for the Greeks, and John for those who were already believers. The standard works on New Testament introduction provide more information on the unique purpose and characteristics of each of the Gospels.[1]

Jesus was a faithful Jew of the first century Who lived in obedience to the Law of God. This meant that

He participated in several of the feasts mandated in the Old Testament. His words and actions on these particular occasions are full of meaning that can only be appreciated if we understand the meaning of the feast that was taking place at the time. We will examine the significance of each feast on the occasions when Jesus participated in it based upon the reconstruction of the life of Jesus. Following you will find more information on why we as believers should learn more about these feasts derived from the Old Testament and Israel's history.

Four Messianic Miracles

Jesus performed so many miracles, but why did the Pharisees react more to some than others? This is a valid question for which there is a reasonable answer. Some time prior to the coming of Jesus, the rabbis divided miracles into two separate categories—those that anyone could perform if empowered to do so by God and those reserved only for the Messiah.

Basically, what happened was that when the rabbis or the Pharisees were asked about specific miracles they could not perform, they would simply tell the people these were miracles only the Messiah could do when He arrived on the scene. Perhaps this explains why the Pharisees were often present when Jesus did a miracle.

We have to remember that in the first century Israel was desperately waiting for the Messiah. They had been under the rule of an oppressor almost from their inception as a nation. If it wasn't the Egyptians, it was the Assyrians or the Babylonians, and if not them, then it was the Romans. The Israelites were tired of being ruled by others and they were waiting and longing for their promised Messiah to set them free.

We need to try to comprehend what was going on in thc mind of a person living in first-century Israel in order to understand what the Israelites were going through as a people. They were expecting a leader who would lead them in an uprising against the Romans, a man who would pave the way for a successful war of liberation. In their desperation for freedom, they forgot that the real purpose of the Messiah was to bring salvation to all Israel.

Every time there was a possible candidate for the Messiah, it was standard procedure to dispatch a group of Pharisees to interview the person and check him out. They even went to John the Baptist because the people were saying that he was the prophet whom Moses said God would send (John 1:19–28).

Every time a Messianic miracle was accomplished, the Pharisees immediately went to investigate. You can rest assured that every time someone performed a Messianic miracle there was great anticipation in the Pharisees' hearts as they went out to investigate the report. No doubt they said among themselves, "Maybe this one will be Him! Maybe He will be the Messiah!"

Invariably they would be disappointed, because that candidate would only perform one of the four necessary miracles required of the Messiah. Then Jesus of Nazareth appeared on the scene. He didn't just perform one Messianic miracle, or two, or three, but He performed all four!

The authorities had to either conclude He was the Messiah or else reject Him because of jealousy and have Him put to death in order to prevent the people from following Him and abandoning their religious way of life. All of these four miracles—healing a leper, casting out a mute demon, healing a man born blind, and raising someone from the dead after four days—will be examined in the order in which they occurred.

The Feasts of the Lord (Lev. 23:1–44)

For many believers, the first question is always: "Why should we as the Gentile church have anything to do with the feasts?" Many people often call these the Feasts of Israel or the Jewish Feasts. The bottom-line question is: "Whose feasts are they anyways?" To answer this question we need to look at Leviticus 23:1–2: "The Lord said to Moses, 'Speak to the Israelites and say to them: "These are my appointed feasts, the appointed feasts of the Lord, which you are to proclaim as sacred assemblies."'" Notice that God did not call them the Feasts of Israel but the "feasts of the Lord." He didn't limit them to a group of people or to a particular period of time. He said they were His feasts, His appointed times.

God has a system. He has a strategic way of doing

things. As Israel celebrated the feasts each year, they were reminded of what God had done for them in the past, but they were also given instructions. He gave the feasts to His people in order to help them understand both who He is and how He moves in history. The feasts are not just about something that happened to Israel thousands of years ago. They are for us today. They have not only historic and theological meaning but also prophetic significance. They point to the Messiah, both to His first and second coming.

The Hebrew word that is used for "sacred assembly" in the passage from Leviticus quoted earlier is *miqra*. Literally it means "rehearsal." The other Hebrew word used in this text is the word for feasts: *mo'ed*. It means "appointed time." So what is the Lord saying to us about His feasts? He is saying that they are rehearsals for appointed times, that they have an important message not just about the past but also about what He has planned for the future.

A clear example of this can be found in the Feast of Passover. The original lamb sacrificed at Passover was literally a "rehearsal" to prepare Israel for their true sacrificial "Lamb," Who was Christ. The Bible teaches that the feasts were shadows of things to come. The Apostle Paul says it clearly in Colossians 2:16–17: "Therefore do not let anyone judge you by what you eat or drink, or with regard to a religious festival, a New Moon celebration or a Sabbath day. These are a shadow of the things that were to come; the reality, however, is found in Christ."

There are three ways in which we can look at our

attitude toward the biblical feasts. Consider the following three words: "could," "should," and "must." As people who are grafted into spiritual Israel we *could* participate in the celebration of the biblical feasts (Rom. 11:17). As we come to understand that the feasts point the way to the Messiah, we can joyfully enter in and make them a part of our lives. As we examine the Scriptures and we see that Jesus faithfully kept the feasts, we might even be prepared to say that we *should* keep the feasts. This also is an acceptable biblical position. Many in the early church celebrated the Feasts of the Lord. Where the danger lies is in the final area, where some would say that we *must* keep the feasts. Like Baptism, keeping the feasts is not a requirement for salvation, but rather, it is something we can choose to do out of a natural outflow of our heart. Every time we celebrate the feasts we are preparing ourselves for their prophetic fulfillment in the glorious return of Christ.

As believers in Christ there is so much for us to glean from the feasts. They not only point to the Messiah; they are actually fulfilled in Him. There are basically four aspects to the feasts that we will cover in this book. First, what was the nature of the feasts? Second, what did the feasts tell the people about the Messiah? Third, as the Messiah, how did Jesus fulfill them? And, fourth and finally, what do the feasts say to us as the church today?

The church has been crying out to God for many years for revival. Many revivals have come and gone. Some have brought much fruit and great results to the body of Christ. One of the key elements to revival is in understanding our Hebraic roots. We have to get back to seeing and worshiping God as the first-century believers did. How did they see God and how did they worship Him?

I believe that New Testament patterns and practices will bring New Testament results. Everyone wants to see an outpouring of the Holy Spirit as in the Book of Acts. The key to the explosive events that took place on the Day of Pentecost is in understanding the Feast of Pentecost. How did three thousand men come to accept Jesus as the Messiah that day? Why were they there? How was it that these men who only a few weeks before rejected Jesus were now ready to confess Him as Savior? Well, we'd better not jump ahead just yet. I will cover that feast in great detail in the final chapters of the book.

The Scriptures are replete with examples of Jesus keeping the feasts. We know that He celebrated the Passover with His disciples every year (Matt. 26:18). He attended the Feast of Unleavened Bread (Mark 14:12). He made His most powerful Messianic claims during the Feast of Tabernacles (John 7:37). Nowhere in all of Scripture are we told to stop celebrating the feasts. In fact, the opposite is true. The Apostle Paul told the Gentile believers in the early church to keep the feasts (1 Cor. 5:7–8). If Jesus kept the feasts and Paul tells us as Gentiles to observe them, why don't we keep and celebrate them today? This is a valid question.

The feasts were God's way of teaching His people

about Himself. If they are God's teaching methods for us, then why are we not using them? How can we understand God and His plans by using our natural minds and by using our own plans? In order to better comprehend the things of God, the Western church needs to go through a radical transformation in these last days.

The feasts demonstrate for us as well as remind us of God's supernatural intervention in the lives of His people. Every time we celebrate the feasts we are reminded of God's activity within humanity. They are a way of instructing our children. When they ask why we celebrate the feasts, we then implement God's pattern for education by providing an explanation for the custom. The feasts show us God's design for salvation. They are the building blocks that contain within themselves the blueprints to helping us identify the Messiah, His Son, Jesus of Nazareth. The feasts can also be described as God's prophetic calendar. They tell us of events past and of events to come.

Many of God's people fall into one of two categories when it comes to feelings about the end times. They are either fearful or confused. God's desire, however, has never been for His children to live in fear or confusion. As we begin to examine and understand the prophetic nature of the feasts, something wonderful happens. Confusion is replaced with clarity, and fear melts away in the presence of total joy. The Rapture becomes an exciting, joyous time, not a strange and scary event to anticipate with dread. As you begin to understand your position as a member of His Bride, the Rapture, second coming, and Millennial reign of Christ are seen in an entirely new light.

The Spring Holidays—Passover, Unleavened Bread, Firstfruits, and Pentecost—all point to events concerning the first coming of Jesus. The Fall Holidays—Trumpets, Day of Atonement, and Tabernacles—all point to events surrounding the second coming of Jesus. It's important for us to note that Jesus fulfilled the first four feasts during His first coming on their respective days. He didn't fulfill them around the days, but He fulfilled them on their actual historic days. If He fulfilled the first four on their actual days, then I would suggest it is reasonable to presume He will fulfill the last three on their actual days. Jesus said we would not know the day or the hour, but we would know the seasons. As we understand the feasts from a first-century perspective and as we celebrate them from a Hebrew cultural point of view, prophecy takes on a fascinating as well as an exciting dimension.

Those who stand in opposition to celebrating the feasts today argue that in Christ our salvation is complete and we no longer need to observe such ancient cultural rituals. It is certainly true that we should never celebrate the feasts in order to achieve or augment our salvation. That was never God's intent for the feasts. He gave them as a vehicle for humanity to find salvation in His Messiah. We don't celebrate the feasts to impress God or to try to win His favor. We celebrate them because it reminds us of what He has done for us and what He is going to do.

The feasts are like memorials or anniversaries. They

are pictures for us, annual reminders of great events. Just like in our lives, when we get out an old photo album and we begin to reminisce about former events, we can't help but smile and sometimes laugh when we look at things we used to wear, hairstyles of days past, and so forth. We see how kids and grown-ups have changed. So, too, when we celebrate the feasts we smile and are filled once again with worship for Almighty God. They take us back to that place of wonder and cause us to see the awesomeness of our great God and King Who stepped down out of heaven into our world and forever changed humanity.

The Early Church and the Feasts

Despite the fact that all of the first believers were Jews, at some point in time there came a separation between the early believers and their Jewish roots. After all, Jesus was a Jewish rabbi who grew up in a Jewish home. As far as the Scriptures tell us, He kept all the requirements of the Torah. We know that He celebrated the feasts annually and so did His earthly parents. His disciples kept them and so did the early church. It's important to emphasize that the early church was predominantly made up of Jewish believers. In the Book of Acts, when Peter stood up to address the crowd in chapter 2, Jewish men present had gathered in Jerusalem to celebrate the Feast of Pentecost. Pentecost was what was called a pilgrim feast. Every male was required by the Lord to travel three times a year to the Temple in Jerusalem to celebrate the feasts. The three pilgrim feasts were Passover, Pentecost, and Tabernacles. So the Temple was filled with tens of thousands of Jewish pilgrims from all over the then-known world when the Day of Pentecost took place.

Let's examine the roots of the early church. We use the term "church" quite normally when we speak of the Book of Acts, but the word "church" didn't come into use until around AD 325. We really should be referring to them as the early believers. These believers, as we have seen from the pilgrim feasts, were Jewish men and their families. A group of twelve Jewish men preached a message about the Jewish Messiah to a gathered throng of Jewish men in the holy city of Jerusalem. It's quite clear that Jewish practices and ideas would have influenced these early believers. Just imagine what it must have been like for them.

For thousands of years they had been celebrating these feasts as a people, always in observance and in obedience to the commands of God. They knew that one day God would fulfill His promises and send them a deliverer, a Messiah. And now they had come to faith in Jesus of Nazareth as their Messiah and all of a sudden all of the symbolism and imagery fell to the side as they saw the fulfillment of the feasts now in Jesus. What an incredible time to be alive!

To begin with, all the believers were Jews. In fact, God had to convince the early church leaders that the Gentiles could come to Jesus on the basis of faith alone by means of a supernatural vision (see Acts 10 and

11). In Acts 15 the church met to discuss this issue and decided that indeed Gentiles could become part of the church on the basis of faith, without the need for circumcision. Within perhaps a decade or two after the Day of Pentecost, there were groups of Jews and Gentiles worshiping together in their local house churches. This explains why the New Testament epistles contain lots of advice on how to work out the different cultural practices between Jewish and Gentile believers in the same church. These included dietary issues, the celebration of special days, and so forth. For an example of this read Romans 14 and 15. In Ephesians 2:11–22 Paul provides clear teaching on the relationship between Jews and Gentiles and how God has joined them together into "one new man" or body in Christ in the church. In the first century then it is evident that the Jew and the Gentile worshiped the Lord together through their newfound faith in the Messiah Jesus.

As the early church progressed into the second century, things began to change drastically. Gentile believers now greatly outnumbered Jewish believers in the church. As a result of this explosion of the Gentile membership, the early church began the process of what has come to be called de-Judaizing. There arose great resentment toward Jewish culture and the traditions of Jewish believers. Things that had been accepted before were no longer tolerated. Customs Jewish believers had been practicing for years were now frowned upon by non-Jewish believers. In this we can see the origins of modern anti-Semitism.

At the same time, the church became more and more influenced by other cultures. Namely, Roman and the Greek ways of thinking had begun to replace Jewish or Hebrew mind-sets. As a result even the biblical holidays were changed. The Passover observance became what is now known as Easter, a name derived from the pagan goddess Ishtar. The Council of Laodicea in AD 365 forbade believers from resting on the Sabbath (Saturday) because in so doing they were Judaizing it.[2]

Well into the third century, Jewish influence in the church was nearly extinct. There were Jewish believers, but their practices and ways of understanding the Scriptures were no longer welcome in the church. Under the rule of the emperor Constantine the Great (272–337) everything began to change. Things that were once accepted were no longer allowed to continue.

Before Constantine, the Gentile believers in the Jewish Messiah, Jesus, were persecuted and sometimes killed for their faith. After Constantine, Gentile believers were no longer persecuted because Constantine converted to Christianity in AD 325 and established it as the official religion of the Roman Empire. Many other pagan religions existed at that time and as we will see their influences crept into the church.

As the church progressed, things got better for the Gentile believers but got progressively worse for the Jewish believers in Messiah Jesus. Any Jews living in that day who came to believe in Jesus of Nazareth as their Messiah were forced to disassociate themselves from Judaism and everything Jewish. Laws were passed that forbade the Jewish believers in Jesus from keeping the biblical Sabbath. They were forbidden to circumcise their sons and they were even forbidden to keep the biblical holidays such as Passover. Punishment for Jewish believers who reverted to Jewish practices included imprisonment and even death. After Constantine banned the biblical holidays he replaced them with pagan holidays derived from other religions.[3]

As we can see from this very brief overview, the celebration of the biblical feasts in the church was rejected by man, not by God. Remember that it was God Who told Moses to instruct Israel to keep the Passover. During the Last Supper, Jesus told His disciples that the bread and wine at the Passover meal pointed to Him and they should remember this whenever they celebrated this feast. I would suggest that if God gave His people the feasts, only God has the right to take them away.

Some have made the mistake of saying that because Jesus already fulfilled the feasts they are no longer valid or appropriate for us to celebrate. That kind of reasoning just doesn't make sense. Just because something has already happened does not make it of any less value or importance. Celebrating the feasts can bring us encouragement and peace, knowing that Jesus did what He said He would do. And because He fulfilled the requirements and the prophecies of His first coming, we know that He will fulfill and do all that is predicted of Him at His second coming.

Many books and articles have been written on the topic of the feasts. The historic and agricultural background has been researched and represented in an excellent manner by many authors. It is not the objective of this work to reiterate what has already been done. The goal of this book is to bring fresh insight into the prophetic nature of the feasts as they depict the life, death, resurrection, and return of the Messiah.

A Note on Sources

This book has been four years in the making. When I started writing this in Israel, it was only meant to be a little booklet that I could use to put on my resource table. I wrote it because so many people were so hungry to learn more about the Hebraic roots of the Christian faith. As time went on and I kept gathering information and researching, it became increasingly clear that it needed to become a book. To that end, there are countless people who have contributed to the information contained within its pages.

Every attempt has been made to provide references for sources wherever possible. When it comes to studying Hebraic roots, we need to be mindful of the fact that the practice of oral tradition is very much a part of the Jewish culture. So much of what is unknown to us as non-Jews is almost common knowledge to a person who has been raised in the land of Israel. It cannot be stressed enough that oral tradition can contribute so much to our understanding of the biblical narrative. I'm grateful to the many Israeli tour guides, rabbis, and pastors who have taught me so much.

I remember as I began to research and prepare for the writing of this book how excited and blown away I was as I discovered many of the truths that you are about to discover. Allow thousands of years of history and tradition to enrich your understanding of the life and teachings of Jesus.

> This is what the LORD Almighty says: "In those days ten men from all languages and nations will take firm hold of one Jew by the hem of his robe and say, 'Let us go with you, because we have heard that God is with you.'" (Zech. 8:23)

Chapter 1

Jesus and John

The story of Jesus begins with the birth of the forerunner, John the Baptist. He is the one sent by God to "make ready a people prepared for the Lord" (Luke 1:17 NASB).

The Birth of John the Baptist

One of the most influential people in the New Testament is Jesus' cousin, John the Baptist. We know of his ministry in his adult years, yet very little if anything is known about his birth or early years. Some scholars speculate that John belonged to the Essenes, a sect of highly religious men who lived an extremely strict and exclusive lifestyle in the wilderness of the Judean desert. The Essenes are believed to have written the now famous Dead Sea Scrolls. They placed high value on baptism or immersion in water for spiritual purification. Some suggest for this reason that John may have belonged to the Essenes in his youth. The jury, however, is still out on this issue.

Why is it important to understand John's birth? The reason is that Luke 1:26 indicates there were six months between the conception of John and the conception of Jesus. If their conceptions were six months apart, then their births would also be approximately six months apart. To understand the date of Jesus' birth, therefore, we must correctly establish the date of John the Baptist's birth. Millions of Christians all over the world celebrate the birthday of Jesus on December 25. We call it Christmas. While most believers enjoy the holiday break and the opportunity to get together with family and exchange gifts, they would admit that December 25 is not likely the actual date on which Jesus was born.

The question is, do we have anything to shed some light on the time of John's birth? The answer is yes. Consider Luke 1:5: "In the time of Herod king of Judea there was a priest named Zechariah, who belonged to the priestly division of Abijah; his wife Elizabeth was also a descendant of Aaron." John the Baptist's father, Zechariah, belonged to the priestly division of Abijah. Luke 1:8–13 tells us that Zechariah was serving in the Temple when he received the news that Elizabeth was with child. Why does Luke mention the fact that Zechariah belonged to the priestly division of Abijah? Do we really care? Should we? I think so. It is important to pay attention to the details of Scripture. God did not fill the Bible with useless information. What at first glance may seem irrelevant or unimportant becomes very relevant once the Jewish cultural background is taken into consideration.

Luke's mention of Abijah is a direct reference to the division of the priests into orders found in 1 Chronicles 24:10. There it is stated that Zechariah's priestly division, Abijah, was the eighth division to serve at the Temple. The Mishnah (Oral Torah) states that each division had to serve twice in one year (but not consecutively), with the first division starting on the first week of Nissan.[1]

Each division served a one-week period and all priestly divisions had to serve during the three pilgrim Festivals. The following is the order of the priestly divisions in relation to the feasts:

- First week of Nissan, the first priestly division of Jehoiarib serves
- Second week of Nissan, second priestly division of Jedaiah serves
- Third week of Nissan, Passover/Feast of Unleavened Bread, *all the priests serve*
- Fourth week of Nissan, third priestly division of Harim serves
- First week of Iyar, fourth priestly division of Seorin serves
- Second week of Iyar, fifth priestly division of Malkijah serves
- Third week of Iyar, sixth priestly division of Mijamin serves
- Fourth week of Iyar, seventh priestly division of Hakkoz serves

- First week of Sivan, eighth priestly division of Abijah serves
- Second week of Sivan, Shavuot (Pentecost), *all the priests serve* (including the division of Abijah), and so on

As a member of the order of Abijah, Zechariah served during the first week of Sivan and then was required to serve the following week for Shavuot (Pentecost). After his service in the Temple, Zechariah went home to his wife. Therefore, John the Baptist must have been conceived some time after Shavuot. Following this logic through, then John the Baptist would have been born in the month of Nissan, the month in which the Festival of Passover is to be observed. Keep in mind that the Scriptures say that John's and Jesus' birthdays are six months apart (Luke 1:26–36). If John was born around Nissan 15, during Passover, then Jesus would have to be born on or near Tishri 15, which happens to be the first day of the biblical Feast of Tabernacles.

One further note of interest about John being born during Passover: The Rabbis teach that the prophet Elijah will appear at Passover to declare Who the Messiah will be. That is why an empty seat is left for Elijah at the head table during the Passover Seder. A child is released to the front door to see if Elijah has come to declare the Messiah. Jesus alluded to John serving in the role of Elijah in Matthew 11:13–15: "For all the Prophets and the Law prophesied until John. And if you are willing to accept it, he is the Elijah who was to come. He who has ears, let him hear." In other words,

John was born during the Passover, precisely the season when the rabbis expected the forerunner of the Messiah to come.

I have established that it is possible that Jesus was born on or near the first day of the Feast of Tabernacles. Perhaps then it is more than a coincidence that the disciple John starts his Gospel by saying, "The Word became flesh and made his dwelling among us" (John 1:14). The Greek word John uses for "made his dwelling" literally means that the Word of God "tabernacled" among men.

This would seem to be a typically Jewish way of suggesting the season in which Jesus was born. This is called the Remez method of teaching, by means of dropping subtle hints. In this style of writing and teaching you don't come right out and make your point, but you lead your audience to the edge of the discovery and allow them to make the connection for themselves and have their own "Aha!" moment. As we look at these Scriptures within a Jewish context, it is very possible that taken together they tell us Jesus was born in the fall, during the Feast of Tabernacles. But there is more.

All of us have the Nativity scene clearly engraved in our minds. There is Mary and Joseph and the baby Jesus surrounded by shepherds, the three wise men, and a few sheep and cows. The scene appears on many Christmas cards and we can see it as we drive by churches during Christmas. If we examine the Scriptures carefully, however, we can see that this is not an entirely accurate picture. Take the three kings for instance. They didn't appear until much later in Jesus' life, we are never told how many there are, and we are never told that they were kings. You can check for yourself in Luke 2:16–20.

One element of the birth scene that we know is correct is the place where Jesus was born. It was a place built to shelter animals from the elements while they slept. According to Luke 2:7, Jesus is placed in a manger. Traditionally this is understood to be a box where feed is placed for the animals. It was placed inside a shed or cave. In Luke 13:15 this same Greek word for "manger" refers to a stall or the entire shelter. In Genesis 33:17 we read: "Jacob, however, went to Succoth, where he built a place for himself and made shelters for his livestock. That is why the place is called Succoth." The Hebrew word *succoth* means "a shelter." It is also the Hebrew name for the Feast of Tabernacles or Feast of Booths, because the people were commanded to build temporary structures to live in to remind them of their time in the wilderness living in tents (Lev. 23:34, 42, 43).

The imagery is staggering when you stop and think about it. The Feast of Tabernacles is all about remembering that during the wilderness journey in Exodus God came to tabernacle or make His dwelling with the Israelites. He was with them in a pillar of fire by night and a pillar of cloud by day. His presence was in their midst in the Tabernacle. Jesus was born around the time of the Feast of Succoth, or shelters, and placed into a manger or shelter by his mother. John in turn tells us that this Jesus is God the Word come to dwell or tabernacle among us for a time just as God came to live among the Israelites in the wilderness. What amazing timing for the birth of Jesus. He temporarily leaves the glory of heaven to come to earth and to pay the price for mankind. He dwells among us temporarily in order to reveal Who God is and to make it possible for God to be in the hearts of His people forever. What a thought!

The Birth of Jesus

One of the cultural insights that helps us in understanding a significant passage concerning the birth of Jesus is found in Luke 2:12: "And this shall be a sign unto you; Ye shall find the babe wrapped in swaddling clothes, lying in a manger" (KJV). This verse refers to the announcement of the angels to the shepherds about the birth of the Messiah. Basically, the angels were giving the shepherds a sign that would help them identify the newborn baby.

What's important to understand about this passage is the cultural implication of the term "swaddling clothes." Most parents when they think of a swaddling cloth used today to wrap a newborn baby think of the typical baby's blanket. However, as we understand a cultural practice from Jesus' time, we come to see this term in a new and exciting light. The practice of that day, and one that continues in some Middle Eastern cultures today, was that if you were to go on a lengthy journey, you would bring with you special strips of cloth that were used for wrapping a dead body. Other translations of Luke 2:12 actually say "strips of cloth." This was the custom so that if you were to die while on the journey you would be wrapped in the strips of cloth to prepare your body for burial.

We know that Joseph and Mary were on a long journey because of the census being taken at the time. Joseph would have had his burial cloth along with him and that was what Jesus was wrapped in at His birth. A swaddling cloth was only used to wrap that which was dead. This provides us with a powerful picture. We know that Jesus was born to be the Lamb of God Who would die for the sins of the world. Even in His birth Jesus was marked by His Father for His life's purpose in death.

The Baptism of Jesus

The New Testament tells us almost nothing about what Jesus was like growing up. We get a brief glimpse of Him in the Temple at age twelve, asking the teachers questions and surprising them with His understanding (Luke 2:41–52). This in itself suggests that the Gospel writers saw His life and, in particular, His death and resurrection as the keys to His significance. At some point around the age of thirty, Jesus begins His ministry by going to John for baptism. Here is Luke's account:

> When all the people were being baptized, Jesus was baptized too. And as he was praying, heaven was opened and the Holy Spirit descended on him in bodily form like a dove. And a voice came from heaven: "You are my Son, whom I love; with you I am well pleased." (Luke 3:21–22)

I've always wondered when I read about Jesus' baptism and a voice coming from heaven why no one, seemingly, responds or reacts to it. How would we react if we heard the audible voice of God in a large meeting or a public place? Would we not be astonished or maybe even afraid? Yet seemingly the people who were present at the baptism heard the voice and had no reaction. Why is this? Again, we turn to first-century Jewish culture to help us understand this most key event in the life and ministry of Jesus. The voice from heaven didn't declare anything new but in fact quoted two very powerful Scriptures that had Messianic implications.

The first Scripture is Psalms 2:7: "I will proclaim the decree of the Lord: He said to me, 'You are my Son; today I have become your Father.'" The second Scripture is Isaiah 42:1: "Here is my servant, whom I uphold, my chosen one in whom I delight; I will put my Spirit on him and he will bring justice to the nations."

God's voice, in those days, was known as the *bat kol*, meaning "daughter of a voice." The rabbinic experts taught that this "echo voice" from heaven was frequently heard among the ancient Israelites after the era of the biblical prophets had ended in the middle of the fifth century BC with the ministry of Malachi. The *bat kol* had become the primary means of communication from God to His people. Saul Lieberman comments, "Sometimes an echo voice, referred to in rabbinic texts as a daughter voice, bat kol, was likened to the sound of a chirping bird or the cooing of a dove."[2]

With this knowledge now we can understand why the crowd did not react the way we might today. God was using a method of communication that was known to the people in that time. Luke tells us he carefully researched many eyewitness (and therefore Jewish) sources (Luke 1:1–4). These Jewish sources would not have explained the *bat kol* because they already understood what took place at the baptism of Jesus. It is we, geographically and historically removed from the culture of Israel, who need the stories behind the stories to help us in our understanding of Jesus.

Chapter 2

The Ministry in Galilee

Following His baptism and temptation in the wilderness, Jesus returns home to Galilee, calls some of His disciples, and then attends the Passover in Jerusalem. He then goes back to Galilee and begins to preach in places such as Capernaum. Then He comes to His hometown of Nazareth and preaches for the first time in the synagogue where He grew up.

In the Nazareth Synagogue

> He went to Nazareth, where he had been brought up, and on the Sabbath day he went into the synagogue, as was his custom. And he stood up to read. The scroll of the prophet Isaiah was handed to him. Unrolling it, he found the place where it is written: "The Spirit of the Lord is on me, because he has anointed me to preach good news to the poor. He has sent me to proclaim

> freedom for the prisoners and recovery of sight for the blind, to release the oppressed, to proclaim the year of the Lord's favor." Then he rolled up the scroll, gave it back to the attendant and sat down. The eyes of everyone in the synagogue were fastened on him. (Luke 4:11–20)

If we look at this passage in greater detail, many customs from the first century begin to emerge. We read that Jesus "went into the synagogue, as was his custom." This is because He was an observant Jewish male. We know from this passage that He didn't just make a onetime or a special appearance at synagogue that week, but it was a normal part of His life.

Then we read that Jesus stood up to read and was handed the scroll of the prophet Isaiah. In the first century and even to this day there is a standardized list for the Torah portions that are read in the synagogue each week. The Torah consists of the first five books of the Bible: Genesis, Exodus, Leviticus, Numbers, and Deuteronomy. These first five books are also known as the books of Moses and they have been and are the foundation and the heartbeat of the Jewish faith, both in ancient times and today.

Along with the weekly Torah portions, there were also the weekly Haf Torah portions, which consisted of readings from the books of the various prophets. Keeping in mind that there were preselected weekly readings in place, we can now understand why Luke says that the scroll of the prophet Isaiah was handed to Jesus. This was because Isaiah was the Haf Torah reading portion for that specific week. Jesus didn't get to pick up a random scroll and choose whatever He wanted to read that week. It was chosen for Him.

Some have tried to suggest that Jesus seized this opportunity to read a very strong Messianic passage to announce His claim as Messiah. However, in light of what we have just learned, we know that this was not thc casc. Furthermore, what stands out in Luke's passage is the reaction of the crowd. The text simply says that after Jesus finished reading the passage He sat down and "the eyes of everyone in the synagogue were fastened on him." It has been suggested by some that the reason everyone was looking at Him was because of His statement that this passage from Isaiah referred to Him. If you look at the text, however, that is not what happened. When Jesus sat down He had not yet made the statement found in Luke 4:21b: "Today this scripture is fulfilled in your hearing." So if they weren't reacting to His statement, then what were they reacting to? To understand the answer to this question, we need to go back to the first century and learn how a synagogue service was structured.

After the two readings of Scripture, the reader was then given the opportunity to make comments about the text that had just been read. This was known as Dvar Torah. It was a sermon or talk on a Torah passage. As in churches today, the reading of the text and the preaching of the Word was done from the podium. Keep this in mind as you think about how after Jesus hands back the scroll He sits down and then proceeds to the Dvar Torah. The question begging to be asked is: "Where did He sit?" Once we know the answer to that question, we will understand why everyone in the synagogue was staring at Him.

At the front of the synagogue in Nazareth, as was also customary in other synagogues, there was a seat known as the Seat of Moses. This was the seat of authority and prominence in the synagogue. Jesus refers to this seat later on in His ministry in Matthew 23:2: "The teachers of the law and the Pharisees sit in Moses' seat." Only the rabbi of that synagogue was permitted to sit and teach from there.

This seat was a very sacred place within the Jewish culture. It was called the Seat of Moses because it was believed that this is where the Messiah, Who was also known as the Second Moses, would sit. That being the case, there was only one place Jesus could have sat at the front of the Nazareth synagogue: the Seat of Moses. In light of this, it's no wonder that people were staring. By the very act of sitting in that seat, Jesus was declaring that He was the Messiah. His words "Today this scripture is fulfilled in your hearing" confirm this, because the Scripture He read spoke of what the Messiah would do when He came. In effect, by both His words and His actions, Jesus was saying, "I am the Messiah!"

The First Messianic Miracle—Healing a Leper

Following the encounter in the Nazareth synagogue,

Jesus probably called Peter, Andrew, James, and John to be His disciples and then did some ministry in Capernaum, where He encountered a leper.

> A man with leprosy came to him and begged him on his knees, "If you are willing, you can make me clean." Filled with compassion, Jesus reached out his hand and touched the man. "I am willing," he said. "Be clean!" Immediately the leprosy left him and he was cured. Jesus sent him away at once with a strong warning: "See that you don't tell this to anyone. But go, show yourself to the priest and offer the sacrifices that Moses commanded for your cleansing, as a testimony to them." Instead he went out and began to talk freely, spreading the news. As a result, Jesus could no longer enter a town openly but stayed outside in lonely places. Yet the people still came to him from everywhere. (Mark 1:40–45)

Jesus is approached by a man with leprosy.[1] As Mark describes it, the man fell before Jesus and asked to be made clean. This sets the stage for His first Messianic miracle.

The Law stated that a person would be defiled by touching a leper. You would also become ceremonially unclean or defiled by touching a dead human body, a dead animal, or a live, unclean animal such as a pig. Lepers were required to keep their distance from others and even to stand downwind from them. They were not allowed to come within the gates of a city. If they were coming close to people, they had to shout

out, "Unclean, unclean!" In fact, they were not permitted to have any human contact with nonlepers (Lev. 13:45, 46).

The Jews considered leprosy a curse from God because of sin in your life or sin in the lives of your parents. Because they believed that only God could forgive sin, they therefore believed only God could heal a person of leprosy. This led to the belief that one day the Messiah would come and do this very miracle.

The passage in Mark 1:40–45 describes this very thing. It is surprising that the man even dared to approach Jesus. We know that he had faith in Christ's power to heal him because he declares, "If you are willing, you can make me clean" (Mark 1:40). His only question was, Are You willing? The response of Jesus is immediate: He reaches out and touches the leper as He heals him. When we realize what leprosy meant to Jews in the first century, it is amazing to realize that for the Messiah leprosy was not something to be avoided lest He become defiled but something to be overcome so that a sufferer could be released from both the pain and the humiliation it brought.

Luke 17:12–14 records another amazing story concerning lepers: "Then as He entered a certain village, there met Him ten men who were lepers, who stood afar off. And they lifted up their voices and said, 'Jesus, Master, have mercy on us!' So when He saw them, He said to them, 'Go, show yourselves to the priests.' And so it was that as they went, they were cleansed" (NKJV).

We can see clearly that these men were in fact lepers

because they were outside the city gates, they shouted from a distance, and no contact was made. In this case, not only does Jesus heal a leper, but He heals ten of them at once! Indeed, as He had proclaimed in the Nazareth synagogue, Jesus came to set the captives free!

"Fence Laws"

Once Jesus began to become known, the Jewish leaders decided He had to be investigated. The Gospels record several incidents where His words or actions were questioned, often by the Pharisees, who were prominent and highly respected Jewish teachers. In this familiar story, as was often the case, they accuse Jesus of violating the ban on working on the Sabbath:

> At that time Jesus went through the grain fields on the Sabbath. His disciples were hungry and began to pick some heads of grain and eat them. When the Pharisees saw this, they said to him, "Look! Your disciples are doing what is unlawful on the Sabbath." He answered, "Haven't you read what David did when he and his companions were hungry? He entered the house of God, and he and his companions ate the consecrated bread—which was not lawful for them to do, but only for the priests. Or haven't you read in the Law that on the Sabbath the priests in the temple desecrate the day and yet are innocent? I tell you that one greater

> than the temple is here. If you had known what these words mean, 'I desire mercy, not sacrifice,' you would not have condemned the innocent. For the Son of Man is Lord of the Sabbath." (Matt. 12:1–8)

Many people use this passage to suggest that Jesus is somehow removing the biblical command to observe the Sabbath. The reason for this is a failure to understand the difference between God's laws and man-made laws known as "fence laws." We know from Scripture that it is impossible that Jesus would ever disobey one of His Father's laws. Jesus states it emphatically in Matthew 5:17–18: "Do not think that I have come to abolish the Law or the Prophets; I have not come to abolish them but to fulfill them. I tell you the truth, until heaven and earth disappear, not the smallest letter, not the least stroke of a pen, will by any means disappear from the Law until everything is accomplished."

So if Jesus isn't referring to the Sabbath law, then what is He referring to? We need to look at the allegations of the Pharisees. Why are they saying He broke the Sabbath? It seems the problem centered upon the disciples' picking the heads of grain. At the time of Jesus, there were various schools of thought about what did and what did not constitute work on the Sabbath. One school of thought would allow the picking of small personal amounts of grain; the other would condemn it. We need to understand that the strict observance of the Torah was the very heartbeat of the Jewish people. They went to great lengths and extremes to keep Torah. There were thousands of what now are known as fence laws.

Here's how fence laws started. When Ezra returned with the people of Israel to Jerusalem from their exile in Babylon, he understood that the Israelites' exile was because of their disobedience to the Torah (Ezra 7:6–10). So in order to prevent that from ever occurring again, he set up the idea of building fences around the original 613 laws of the Torah. You would have to "jump over that fence" (so to speak) or break that fence law before you could actually break the real law. Ezra believed that by doing this he was protecting the Jewish people from future exile.

Over the centuries, so many of these fence laws were added, to the point where there are now in excess of three hundred thousand to five hundred thousand fence laws in orthodox Judaism.[2] For instance, one of God's commands is to keep the Sabbath and to do no work on that day. Out of the Jewish people's strong desire to obey God and to not break a commandment, these other rules and guidelines were put in place. It's important to note that these were put into effect out of good intentions, but with the passing of time the number of fence laws increased to the point that it was nearly impossible to observe them all. With all of these laws in place, it didn't take very long for the people of Israel to fall into the snare of serving the law instead of serving the living God.

So when we look back to the text, in reality Jesus wasn't being accused of breaking the Sabbath; He was being accused of breaking one of their man-made fence laws. Jesus *never* broke God's law. In Galatians 4:4 we see that Jesus, as a first-century Jewish male, was born under the law as were all Jewish men in that time: "But when the time had fully come, God sent his Son, born of a woman, born under law." Every time we see Jesus debating with the Pharisees over conduct or religious observances, we need to remember that He's not discarding the laws and ways of Torah, but He's challenging the rules of man.

Washing the Feet of Jesus

Following the delivery of the Sermon on the Mount, Jesus heals the centurion's slave in Capernaum (Luke 7:1–10) and raises the widow's son in the village of Nain (Luke 7:11–17). Jesus then responds to questions from John's disciples and goes to dine with a Pharisee. Luke picks up the story from there:

> Now one of the Pharisees invited Jesus to have dinner with him, so he went to the Pharisee's house and reclined at the table. When a woman who had lived a sinful life in that town learned that Jesus was eating at the Pharisee's house, she brought an alabaster jar of perfume, and as she stood behind him at his feet weeping, she began to wet his feet with her tears. Then she wiped them with her hair, kissed them and poured perfume on them. (Luke 7:36–38)

Embedded within the words of this story is a deep and profound cultural truth. Most of us who are non-Jewish have the tendency to see the Scriptures through our own particular cultural lenses. This story is a perfect example. On the surface this story provides us with a beautiful example of the compassionate and forgiving heart of Jesus. However, as we look deeper into this passage we can discover more truth.

Have you ever thought about how much water it actually took to wash a person's feet? Do you think it's possible for one woman to cry enough tears at one sitting to do so? Of course not! So how, then, do we explain the fact that there were enough tears that day for this woman to wash Jesus' feet?

In order to understand how this was possible we need to look into an ancient Jewish custom that existed at the time of Jesus. It was common for families to have what was known as a "*lacrima* jar" (*lacrima* from the Latin meaning "tear"). Traditionally these jars were used to keep the tears of families from multiple generations. We know that this tradition existed from at least the time of King David. This is illustrated in Psalms 56:8: "You have taken account of my wanderings; Put my tears in Your bottle. Are they not in Your book?" (NASB).

With this understanding in mind, think of what really took place that day. I'm sure this repentant woman was weeping and that her tears assisted in the washing of Jesus' feet. But how much more powerful is it to consider the possibility that she was pouring out not only her tears but also the tears of hurt and pain from previous generations of her family? Literally all of the pain of generations can be brought to Jesus, the One Who said, "Come to me, all you who are weary and burdened, and I will give you rest" (Matt. 11:28). What a beautiful picture when we consider this cultural implication. In this passage and so many others, the beauty of the verses is brought to light when we understand the cultural traditions and practices behind them.

The Second Messianic Miracle—Casting Out a Mute Demon

Not long after the incident just described, Jesus goes on a preaching tour with the Twelve and a group of women who have been healed and who provided some support for His ministry (Luke 8:1–3). This leads to the following encounter:

> Then they brought him a demon-possessed man who was blind and mute, and Jesus healed him, so that he could both talk and see. All the people were astonished and said, "Could this be the Son of David?" (Matt. 12:22–23)

It's interesting to note that right after this miracle the people began to ask, "Could this be the Son of David?" or in other words, "Could this be the Messiah?" Jesus performed many miracles, so why did this one place Him as a candidate for the position of Messiah? The answer is because it was, in fact, a Messianic miracle and all who were there, Pharisees included, knew it was.

In first-century Israel the rabbis would cast out demons with a particular method. The person who was demon possessed would be brought in before them. The rabbis would then ask the name of the demon and then cast it out using that name. But the problem was that when a mute demon was presented, their method could not work because the mute demon could not speak and so the rabbis could not cast it out. As a result it was said that only the Messiah would have the authority to cast out a mute spirit. That is exactly what Jesus did and why the people were whispering among themselves.

At this point Jesus had performed two of the four expected Messianic miracles. This miracle was a major turning point in the ministry of Jesus. He wasn't just a good teacher anymore; He was being considered as a candidate for the Messiah!

The Tzitzit (Prayer Shawl) Prophecy

Jesus teaches a number of parables on the Kingdom of God (Matt. 13:1–52), calms a storm on the Sea of Galilee (Mark 4:35–41), and heals the Gerasene demoniac (Mark 5:1–20). He is then asked to heal the daughter of Jarius. In the midst of this, a suffering woman reaches out and finds wholeness:

> A large crowd followed and pressed around him. And a woman was there who had been subject to bleeding for twelve years. She had suffered a great deal under the care of many doctors and had spent all she had, yet instead of getting better she grew worse. When she heard about Jesus, she came up behind him in the crowd and touched his cloak, because she thought, "If I just touch his clothes, I will be healed." Immediately her bleeding stopped and she felt in her body that she was freed from her suffering." (Mark 5:25–29)

> And, behold, a woman, which was diseased with an issue of blood twelve years, came behind Him, and touched the hem of His garment." (Matt. 9:20 KJV)

This is a well-known portion of Scripture that has been preached countless times, I'm sure. It is probable that we have all reached the same conclusion—that this was a passage about determination. We need to be like the woman with the issue of blood, press in through the crowds and don't worry about what other people say—just touch Jesus and you will be healed. For the most part, this is the extent to which the passage is understood, and it is a valid and accurate message.

What is important to note about this passage is that according to Matthew's account, she reached for the hem of His garment. Today, what do we consider to be a hem? We probably think of the hem on a skirt or the hems on a pair of pants. Culturally we know this wouldn't be the case with Jesus because during the first century men wore garments that resembled robes.

The Greek word for "hem" here is *kraspedon*, which means "a tassel of twisted wool." Most people have the idea that because the crowds were so great she was happy just to be able to touch any part of the garment. But, in fact, she reached for the tassel at the end of His garment. Why is that important? Why does Matthew draw our attention to the fact that she reached for and touched the tassel on Jesus' garment?[3]

First of all we should identify what it was in fact that Jesus was wearing, keeping in mind that we know that as an observant first-century Jewish male Jesus would have kept the command found in Numbers 15:37–41:

> The Lord said to Moses, "Speak to the Israelites and say to them: 'Throughout the generations to come you are to make tassels on the corners of your garments, with a blue cord on each tassel. You will have these tassels to look at and so you will remember all the commands of the Lord, that you may obey them and not prostitute yourselves by going after the lusts of your own hearts and eyes. Then you will remember to obey all my commands and will be consecrated to your God. I am the Lord your God, who brought you out of Egypt to be your God. I am the Lord your God."

Again the Lord commanded them in Deuteronomy 22:12: "Make tassels on the four corners of the cloak you wear."

Therefore, according to the Scriptures, Jesus was wearing a garment that would resemble a modern-day prayer shawl. It was also known as a tzitzit. In Numbers 15:38, the word translated for "border" or "corner" is the Hebrew word *kanaph*, which is also translated as "wings." Therefore, the corners of the prayer shawl are often called the "wings" of the garment. Each prayer shawl had a tassel on each corner that was made of eight threads and five double knots, which had a total numeric value of thirteen. The Hebraic numerical value for the word "tzitzit" is 600. Add these together and you have a total of 613, which points to the 613 commandments of the law.[4]

Now that we see the picture of wings on the corners of a prayer shawl, we can gain new insight into the moving words of Psalms 91:1–4: "He who dwells in the shelter of the Most High will rest in the shadow of the Almighty. I will say of the Lord, 'He is my refuge and my fortress, my God, in whom I trust.' Surely he will save you from the fowler's snare and from the deadly pestilence. He will cover you with his feathers, and under his wings you will find refuge; his faithfulness will be your shield and rampart." This speaks of being under the covering of God's law and protection. Even to this day, it's commonplace to see a Jewish man during his time of prayer with a prayer shawl completely covering his face. Wearing the prayer shawl like this is a symbolic gesture indicating a person's inward desire not only to be under the law of God but also to literally clothe himself in His law.

Out of this understanding in the first century there developed a belief about the prayer shawl of the Messiah. This belief was that the tassels of the Messiah's garment possessed healing powers.[5] No doubt, this is linked to the Messianic prophecy found in Malachi 4:2: "But unto you that fear my name shall the Sun of righteousness arise with healing in his wings" (KJV). Imagine the implication this had in the first century. What we just read from Malachi contains what is known as a Messianic title ("Sun of Righteousness"). Other examples include "the Bright Morning Star," "the Root of Jesse," "the Son of David," and dozens more.

So if "Sun of Righteousness" is a Messianic title, then Malachi 4:2 is a prophecy about the Messiah. Since Jesus is the Messiah, then this would be a prophecy about Him. Keeping in mind the woman who had the issue of blood, consider how powerful this passage becomes when we insert the name of Jesus for the title "Sun of Righteousness." The passage would read: "But unto you that fear my name shall Jesus arise with healing in his wings."

The woman with the issue of blood lived in first-century Israel and was aware of this prophecy. The text says that she thought to herself that if she just touched the wings of Jesus' garment she would be healed. When she heard that Jesus, Who was possibly the Messiah, was passing by, it would explain why she felt she must touch the hem or tassel on His garment.

The rest of the story is found in Mark 5:30–34. Jesus realizes that power has gone out from Him. He asks His disciples to find out who touched Him. The disciples have no way of knowing because the crowds are pressed up against them, but Jesus insists on knowing who touched Him. The woman comes forward and explains her situation to Jesus. She has had this issue of blood (a hemorrhaging problem) for twelve years. She has spent all her money on doctors only to have her problem become worse with time. At that point Jesus commends her and attributes her healing to her faith in Him. She heard that the Messiah was passing through her town. She believed He was coming with healing in His wings. It was her faith in the fact that Jesus was her long-awaited Messiah that healed her. The tassels themselves had nothing to do with her healing. It was her faith in the person who was wearing the tassels—the Messiah.

Following this incident Jesus continues to the other side of Galilee to seek a time of rest. As Mark 6:53–56 records, "when they had crossed over, they landed at Gennesaret and anchored there. As soon as they got out of the boat, people recognized Jesus. They ran throughout that whole region and carried the sick on mats to wherever they heard he was. And wherever he went—into villages, towns or countryside—they placed the sick in the marketplaces. They begged him to let them touch even the edge of his cloak, and all who touched him were healed." Once again the word used here for edge of His cloak is *kraspedon*, the Greek word for "tassel." Just as the woman with the issue of blood was healed upon touching the tassel of Jesus' garment, all who touched the tassel of His garment were healed.

All Foods Are Clean

Now Jesus has returned to Nazareth, where he sends the Twelve out on a mission (Mark 6; John 6). After they return, the five thousand are fed and Jesus goes back to Gennesaret. He teaches that He is the Bread of Life and many of His disciples turn away from following Him. The Pharisees begin to question the actions of the disciples and, by implication, the teaching of their Master:

> The Pharisees and some of the teachers of the law who had come from Jerusalem gathered around Jesus and saw some of his disciples eating food with hands that were "unclean," that is, unwashed. (The Pharisees and all the Jews do not eat unless they give their hands a ceremonial washing, holding to the tradition of the elders. When they come from the marketplace they do not eat unless they wash. And they observe many other traditions, such as the washing of cups, pitchers and kettles.) So the Pharisees and teachers of the law asked Jesus, "Why don't your disciples live according to the tradition of the elders instead of eating their food with 'unclean' hands?" He replied, "Isaiah was right when he prophesied about you hypocrites; as it is written: 'These people honor me with their lips, but their hearts are far from me. They worship me in vain; their teachings are but rules taught by men.' You have let go of the commands of God and are holding on to the traditions of men." And he said to them:

> "You have a fine way of setting aside the commands of God in order to observe your own traditions! For Moses said, 'Honor your father and your mother,' and, 'Anyone who curses his father or mother must be put to death.' But you say that if a man says to his father or mother: 'Whatever help you might otherwise have received from me is Corban' (that is, a gift devoted to God), then you no longer let him do anything for his father or mother. Thus you nullify the word of God by your tradition that you have handed down. And you do many things like that." Again Jesus called the crowd to him and said, "Listen to me, everyone, and understand this. Nothing outside a man can make him 'unclean' by going into him. Rather, it is what comes out of a man that makes him 'unclean.'" After he had left the crowd and entered the house, his disciples asked him about this parable. "Are you so dull?" he asked. "Don't you see that nothing that enters a man from the outside can make him 'unclean'? For it doesn't go into his heart but into his stomach, and then out of his body." (In saying this, Jesus declared all foods "clean.") He went on: "What comes out of a man is what makes him 'unclean.' For from within, out of men's hearts, come evil thoughts, sexual immorality, theft, murder, adultery, greed, malice, deceit, lewdness, envy, slander, arrogance and folly. All these evils come from inside and make a man 'unclean.'" (Mark 7:1–23)

Traditionally, this passage has been used by many to suggest that Jesus was doing away with all the food laws that God outlined in the Torah. As I mentioned in the section about the fence laws, it's important to note it here again that Jesus was born under the law and that with His own lips He declared that He did not come to abolish the law, but in fact He had come to fulfill it, which in the Hebrew culture means that He came to bring the maximum understanding of the Law.[6]

Notice that it is not the food laws that are in question here, but rather it's the issue of ritual purity and upholding the oral traditions (such as the fence laws). The Pharisees were upset because Jesus' disciples weren't observing the traditional man-made laws of ceremonial cleanliness—they were eating food with hands that were unclean. During the first century, there were regulations and rituals that had to be performed before you began the meal. These Pharisees were of the opinion that if these rituals were not performed before you ate, you would defile the food and make it unclean. Jesus speaks to this issue in verses 1–13. He then turns to the crowds and shares a more general principle as to what causes spiritual defilement, which He later explains in more detail to the disciples in private (vv. 14–23).

This is the context of the statement in verse 19: "In saying this, Jesus declared all foods 'clean.'" The principle is that defilement comes from the sinful desires of our hearts such as sexual immorality, theft, murder, adultery, greed, malice, and deceit. The statement in verse 19 confirms that no food can cause *spiritual* defilement. It is not my position that the eating of unclean animals is a sin. Nothing we eat causes us to be guilty of sin before God. We are no longer bound by the Old Testament dietary laws *as regards maintaining our relationship with God.* That is established through faith in Christ, Who perfectly fulfilled all of God's will on our behalf in His life and carried away our sins by His death and resurrection. This does not mean, however, that the teaching of the Old Testament regarding what we eat is no longer of any value.

The Book of Leviticus provides a list of foods the Jews were expected to avoid (see Lev. 11). These included things such as pork and shellfish. If we understand that God created our bodies and that because He loves His people He wants us to be in the best of health, then we must recognize that He knows what is best for us. The Bible is God's "manual" for how to live the best possible life as a human being.

Think about your car, for example. In most cases the manufacturer's instruction manual says to change the oil every 3,000 miles. You won't ruin the car immediately if you go over the 3,000-mile recommendation, but it won't perform at optimum power and if you continue to neglect to follow this recommendation, over time it will harm the engine. In the same way, I am convinced that God gave us these food laws for our benefit. He wants us to have a long and healthy life. Our decision to follow them or ignore them is determined by our view of God. Do we see Him as mean enough to provide all sorts of tempting foods and then tell us arbitrarily we can't eat them *or* do we know Him as a loving Father Who knows what is best for us and has our best interest at heart?

Here is another illustration. As a parent, if you were to tell your child not to play on the street, they might think you were trying to limit their fun and want to play on the street anyway. In the process, let's say they are struck by a vehicle and injured. As a parent, are you upset with your child or do you love them any less for ignoring your instructions? Of course not! But had they listened to your instructions, they would have remained safe. This is how we should view the food laws. They are there to help us to enjoy life and to live long and healthy lives.

Some might say, "If God didn't want us to eat these animals, then why did He create them?" It's a good question and there's a good answer. Consider what would happen to our oceans if God had not created creatures such as lobsters, shrimp, catfish, oysters, and so forth. They feed on the dead matter from other sea creatures. It's their God-given job to eat all of the rotting, bacteria-infested waste found in our waters. They were created to be God's vacuum cleaners! These creatures play an essential role in keeping our waters clean. If it were not for them, the world's oceans and rivers would be overrun with filth. So we thank God for creating these animals. They play an important role in our ecological system. We need to understand that as the Scriptures indicate, however, not all animals were created for consumption.

Our God is a loving Father Who cares and wants the best for me. I understand that as my creator He knows my body better than anyone else. I also know that He has my best interests at heart. That's why when He gives me advice on my diet I want to pay attention!

Binding and Loosing

Jesus makes a ministry trip to Tyre and Sidon on the Mediterranean coast, where He heals the daughter of the Syrophonecian woman (Matt. 15:21–28). He returns via the Decapolis on the eastern side of the Jordan, feeds the four thousand, then heads for the shores of the Sea of Galilee (Matt. 15:29–39). From there He goes to Caesarea Philippi, where Peter makes his confession of Christ as the Messiah, which sets the stage for the subject of binding and loosing, which is one of the most misunderstood concepts of all the teachings of Jesus. We begin to study this saying by reading the following story:

> When Jesus came to the region of Caesarea Philippi, he asked his disciples, "Who do people say the Son of Man is?" They replied, "Some say John the Baptist; others say Elijah; and still others, Jeremiah or one of the prophets." "But what about you?" he asked. "Who do you say I am?" Simon Peter answered, "You are the Christ, the Son of the living God." Jesus replied, "Blessed are you, Simon son of Jonah, for this was not revealed to you by man, but by my Father in heaven. And I tell you that you are Peter, and on this rock I will build my church, and the gates of Hades

> will not overcome it. I will give you the keys of the kingdom of heaven; whatever you bind on earth will be bound in heaven, and whatever you loose on earth will be loosed in heaven." Then he warned his disciples not to tell anyone that he was the Christ." (Matt. 16:13–20)

This is a historic moment in the lives of both Jesus and Peter. For the first time, Jesus is recognized as the Messiah by one of His own disciples. Equally powerful is the fact that it is Peter who is the first of the disciples to recognize that Jesus is the Messiah. It's a great moment for sure.

What did Jesus mean when He told Peter that whatever he bound on earth would be bound in heaven and whatever he loosed on earth would be loosed in heaven? There are many today who believe that Jesus was giving Peter authority to bind and loose demonic spirits from people. In first-century Israel, however, the words "binding" and "loosing" were legal terms.[7] They were used to make determinations in laws pertaining to unclear commands in the Torah. To "bind" something meant to forbid it, and to "loose" something meant to permit it. For example, the Bible forbids working on the Sabbath but does not give any clear instructions on what would constitute work. As a result many times the rabbis were called upon to settle disputes that would have arisen among the people to determine what would or what would not be defined as work. The rabbis would hear the arguments and then make a decision. If the rabbi determined that what was being stated was considered work, he would then "bind" or forbid that particular activity from being done on the Sabbath. If he felt the activity was not work, then he would "loose" or permit the activity.

Let's take another glance at what Jesus said to Peter: "I will give you the keys of the kingdom of heaven; whatever you bind on earth will be bound in heaven, and whatever you loose on earth will be loosed in heaven." In the light of what that statement meant in first-century Israel, Jesus was giving Peter the authority to make rulings over spiritual matters within the early church.

Basically, Jesus was saying that whatever Peter would decide would be backed up or approved or accepted by heaven. What an awesome responsibility! We see in the Book of Acts a clear example of Peter's authority to bind and loose:

> Then some of the believers who belonged to the party of the Pharisees stood up and said, "The Gentiles must be circumcised and required to obey the law of Moses." The apostles and elders met to consider this question. After much discussion, Peter got up and addressed them: "Brothers, you know that some time ago God made a choice among you that the Gentiles might hear from my lips the message of the gospel and believe. God, who knows the heart, showed that he accepted them by giving the Holy Spirit to them, just as he did to us. He made no distinction between us and them, for he purified their hearts by faith. Now then, why do you try to test God by putting on the

> necks of the disciples a yoke that neither we nor our fathers have been able to bear? No! We believe it is through the grace of our Lord Jesus that we are saved, just as they are." The whole assembly became silent as they listened to Barnabas and Paul telling about the miraculous signs and wonders God had done among the Gentiles through them.
>
> When they finished, James spoke up: "Brothers, listen to me. Simon has described to us how God at first showed his concern by taking from the Gentiles a people for himself. The words of the prophets are in agreement with this, as it is written: 'After this I will return and rebuild David's fallen tent. Its ruins I will rebuild, and I will restore it, that the remnant of men may seek the Lord, and all the Gentiles who bear my name, says the Lord, who does these things' that have been known for ages. It is my judgment, therefore, that we should not make it difficult for the Gentiles who are turning to God. Instead we should write to them, telling them to abstain from food polluted by idols, from sexual immorality, from the meat of strangled animals and from blood." (Acts 15:5–20)

Peter "loosed" the Gentiles from having to be circumcised and keep all the requirements of the Law. James then gave an example of "binding" when he stated four pagan practices that the Gentiles were required to abstain from. We need to recognize that this authority was given not only to Peter but to all the Apostles who formed the foundation of the universal Church according to Ephesians 2:19, 20. This is one of the reasons that the early church only recognized as authoritative books written by an Apostle or the associate of an Apostle. They were given the authority to lay down practical teachings to help the churches walk in the way of the Lord. This means that for us the New Testament, which is based upon their apostolic authority, is the place we must go for true understanding of what it means to follow Jesus.

The Gates of Hades

The story just discussed contains another much misunderstood saying we need to explore, and that concerns "The Gates of Hades":

> When Jesus came to the region of Caesarea Philippi, he asked his disciples, "Who do people say the Son of Man is?" They replied, "Some say John the Baptist; others say Elijah; and still others, Jeremiah or one of the prophets." "But what about you?" he asked. "Who do you say I am?" Simon Peter answered, "You are the Christ, the Son of the living God." Jesus replied, "Blessed are you, Simon son of Jonah, for this was not revealed to you by man, but by my Father in heaven. And I tell you that you are Peter, and on this rock I will build my church, and the gates of Hades will not overcome it." (Matt. 16:13–18)

A working knowledge of Israel's geography and topography is critical in our understanding of many biblical accounts. This is one of those accounts where Bible geography helps us to understand what Jesus was saying to His disciples when He asked them about how others viewed Him.

The text clearly states they were at a place called Caesarea Philippi. Today, in modern Israel, this place is known as Banias. Caesarea Philippi is found at the base of Mount Hermon in the Golan Heights of Israel not far from the borders of western Syria. This, in fact, was the most northern region of Jesus' earthly ministry.

About three hundred years before the time of Jesus, the occupying force in Israel was the Greeks, led by Alexander the Great. When the Greeks conquered another people, they introduced them to their religion. The religion of the Greeks was based upon the stories of Greek mythology. This mythology introduced Israel to the idea of polytheism, the belief in many gods. The Greeks also brought with them views on worship and sacrifice that influenced Israel for a period of three hundred years, right up until the time of Jesus.

The epicenter of activity for the Greeks and this new religion was at Caesarea Philippi. Here existed a large sanctuary built for the purpose of offering human sacrifices to Pan, the Greek god, who was part man and part goat. The legend of Pan told that he would roam through the forests playing his flute (hence the name "pan flute"). It was said the sound of his flute was so terrible that people would run from the forest in absolute terror. That is why to this day we use the term "panic" to express when someone is acutely afraid.

Caesarea Philippi had not only the sanctuary for Pan there but also many gates carved into the rock of Mount Hermon. There was an altar for Zeus and other various Greek gods as well. These altars were called the Gates of Hades. This Greek religion drew many so-called Hellenized Jews into its sphere.

People who followed the Greek religious myths believed that a man who could perform miracles was a god. We can see this clearly in Acts 14:8–13:

> In Lystra there sat a man crippled in his feet, who was lame from birth and had never walked. He listened to Paul as he was speaking. Paul looked directly at him, saw that he had faith to be healed and called out, "Stand up on your feet!" At that, the man jumped up and began to walk. When the crowd saw what Paul had done, they shouted in the Lycaonian language, "The gods have come down to us in human form!" Barnabas they called Zeus, and Paul they called Hermes because he was the chief speaker. The priest of Zeus, whose temple was just outside the city, brought bulls and wreaths to the city gates because he and the crowd wanted to offer sacrifices to them.

Clearly after seeing Jesus' miracles in the region the people must have thought He was some kind of god. That is why in the text we find Jesus asking His disciples, "Who do people say the Son of Man is?"

In the light of this we can now see why Peter's confession was so striking. We also have new insight into why Jesus said what He did to Peter. At the very source of this thriving polytheistic center Jesus says that the Gates of Hades would not prevail against the church. Jesus, in a very powerful way, was saying that the polytheism of the Greeks would not prevail against the monotheism of Israel. He was saying that this power of the false gods of Greek paganism would not overcome His new movement, the church. Jesus wasn't just "*a* god"; He was "*the* God" of Israel—the Messiah. His words have come to pass. Greek mythology has come and gone in the land of Israel, but Christianity has continued to grow to become the world's largest religion. Praise God that the Gates of Hades have not and will not prevail against the church!

The Transfiguration

Following Peter's great confession in Caesarea Philippi, Jesus begins to reveal more of the cost of following Him and of the ultimate price He Himself will have to pay (Matt. 16:21–28). Now that Jesus' three closest disciples, Peter, James, and John, have begun to enter into a more intimate understanding of the Master, Jesus decides it is time to reveal Himself in all His glory to them. Here's Matthew's account:

> Now after six days Jesus took Peter, James, and John his brother, led them up on a high mountain by them-

> selves; and He was transfigured before them. His face shone like the sun, and His clothes became as white as the light. And behold, Moses and Elijah appeared to them, talking with Him. Then Peter answered and said to Jesus, "Lord, it is good for us to be here; if You wish, let us make here three tabernacles: one for You, one for Moses, and one for Elijah." While he was still speaking, behold, a bright cloud overshadowed them; and suddenly a voice came out of the cloud, saying, "This is My beloved Son, in whom I am well pleased. Hear Him!" And when the disciples heard it, they fell on their faces and were greatly afraid. But Jesus came and touched them and said, "Arise, and do not be afraid." When they had lifted up their eyes, they saw no one but Jesus only. Now as they came down from the mountain, Jesus commanded them, saying, "Tell the vision to no one until the Son of Man is risen from the dead." And His disciples asked Him, saying, "Why then do the scribes say that Elijah must come first?" Jesus answered and said to them, "Indeed, Elijah is coming first and will restore all things. But I say to you that Elijah has come already, and they did not know him but did to him whatever they wished. Likewise the Son of Man is also about to suffer at their hands." Then the disciples understood that He spoke to them of John the Baptist. (Matt. 17:1–13 NKJV)

The transfiguration of Jesus is one of the most momentous events in His ministry. The Book of Revelation speaks of two witnesses who will appear at the time of the second coming of the Messiah. The Apostle John gives us very interesting details to help us identify who these two witnesses are. The description is given here in Revelation 11:3–6:

> And I will give power to my two witnesses, and they will prophesy for 1,260 days, clothed in sackcloth. These are the two olive trees and the two lampstands that stand before the Lord of the earth. If anyone tries to harm them, fire comes from their mouths and devours their enemies. This is how anyone who wants to harm them must die. These men have power to shut up the sky so that it will not rain during the time they are prophesying; and they have power to turn the waters into blood and to strike the earth with every kind of plague as often as they want.

Revelation states that the first witness will have the power to shut up the skies so that it will not rain—this refers to none other than the prophet Elijah (see 1 Kings 17:1). The second witness has the power to turn water into blood and release plagues upon the earth. This is an obvious reference to Moses (see Exodus 7). It's important to consider what Revelation says will happen at the second appearing of the Messiah. Isn't it interesting then that it was Elijah and Moses who appeared at the transfiguration at the Messiah's first coming? This is God's way of showing us that Jesus truly was His Messiah.

The timing of the transfiguration may also be strategic. God seems to use the feasts to mark important and historical events. Earlier we saw that the birth of John the Baptist took place most likely during the Feast of Passover and that most likely Jesus was born during the Feast of Tabernacles. It is possible that the transfiguration actually took place during the Feast of Tabernacles. Most people miss this because we don't always appreciate or notice the importance of the festivals. Here in Matthew 17:4 Peter says, "Lord, it is good for us to be here; if You wish, let us make here three tabernacles: one for You, one for Moses, and one for Elijah" (NKJV). Notice what Peter offers to build: three tabernacles (the Amplified Bible says "booths"). This is a reference to the special booths that God commanded Israel to build and live in for seven days during the Feast of Tabernacles. The reference to tabernacles or booths on the part of Peter suggests that the transfiguration of Jesus may have taken place during the Feast of Tabernacles. This is yet another example of why it's important and beneficial for believers to study and understand the feasts.

The Mustard Seed

As Jesus and the three disciples descend the Mount of Transfiguration, they are met with a challenge. There is a demonized boy whom the other disciples have tried to deliver without success. Jesus heals the boy and then the disciples ask why they could not. This brings forth a powerful teaching on the subject of faith.

One of the greatest and most precious of things

we as believers have is the gift of faith. Faith is the very thing that drives us to continue when our circumstances tell us differently. Faith is what gives us hope to persevere against all odds. It is at the core of who we are as followers of Christ. Jesus recognized the importance of having faith and taught His disciples on this key issue. In Matthew 17:20, when the disciples asked Jesus why they could not cast the demon out of a boy, "he replied, 'Because you have so little faith. I tell you the truth, if you have faith as small as a mustard seed, you can say to this mountain, "Move from here to there" and it will move. Nothing will be impossible for you.'"

Many of us have read this passage and have been stirred to levels of great faith because of it. Jesus decides to use a mustard seed in His presentation on how to have faith. Why the mustard seed? At this point in our search to find the historical Jesus we must remind ourselves of some very crucial facts about who He was. Jesus was a rabbi living in Israel in the first century. So as a rabbi, Jesus not only fulfilled the role of a rabbi, but He also used the methods and practices of the rabbis.

One notable example is what I would call the walking and talking method. The rabbis would journey together with their followers for days at a time passing through the hillsides, villages, and cities. As they walked, their students or "disciples" would ask them questions. Being quick on their feet, the rabbis would select something from their current surroundings that would serve as an illustration for their answers. This brings us to Jesus using the mustard seed as an illustration. In understanding the Scriptures, context is everything, and this story is no exception. The story can be found in Matthew 17:14–20:

> He replied, "Because you have so little faith. I tell you the truth, if you have faith as small as a mustard seed, you can say to this mountain, 'Move from here to there' and it will move. Nothing will be impossible for you."

> He said to them, Because of the littleness of your faith [that is, your lack of firmly relying trust]. For truly I say to you, if you have faith [that is living] like a grain of mustard seed, you can say to this mountain, Move from here to yonder place, and it will move; and nothing will be impossible to you. (Matt. 17:20 AMP)

Notice the subtle changes between the two versions. The New International Version says that we are to have faith the size of a mustard seed. The Amplified Version (which takes into consideration Aramaic—the spoken language at the time of Christ) states that we are to have faith that is "living" like a grain of mustard seed. There are two things that we will examine here: (1) What mountain was Jesus referring to in this context? and (2) Why should we have faith that is *living* like a grain of mustard seed?

The first thing we need to understand about this passage is that the word "mountain" used by Jesus was a first-century figure of speech. A "mountain" at that time and within that culture represented a person or thing that held a position of authority. Because of the authority the rabbis held within a community they were often referred to as "mountains." So when two rabbis with opposing views would debate on Torah interpretation, the people would often say, "My mountain is going to crush your mountain." An example of this kind of figurative language is recorded in Ezekiel 36:1: "Son of man, prophesy to the mountains of Israel and say, 'O mountains of Israel, hear the word of the Lord.'" Here we clearly see that the prophet was not speaking to the physical mountains of Israel but rather those who were the rulers and authorities of the land.

The question that needs to be addressed in the Matthew account is: "What mountain is Jesus referring to?" A loving father brings his demonized son to the disciples, who fail in their efforts to cast out the demon. The father then goes directly to Jesus to get the job done. In frustration with His disciples He casts out the demon. Afterward, during a private conversation with His disciples, He teaches them that if their faith can live like a mustard seed, then they will be able to move mountains. The mountain in this scenario would be the demonic powers or authorities afflicting the boy. Jesus is telling His disciples that if their faith has the qualities of a mustard seed, they will be able to move these mountains (demonic powers).

The second question then is: "Why the mustard seed? Why must our faith live like the mustard seed?" The apparent qualities of this mustard seed are so important that Jesus uses it to illustrate our faith. Among those in the farming community (many who heard Jesus made their living by farming) there was a good deal of frustration surrounding the mustard seed. The mustard is actually a weed and it will grow in almost any environment. We should remind ourselves that Jesus is using rabbinic methods. As He looks around he undoubtedly sees mustard plants around Him as He shares this teaching.

Mustard plants were and are all around Israel, both in Jesus' time and in modern times. In fact, I am writing this portion of the book today from my hotel room in Tiberias. Just today as I drove down the highway I saw the roadside covered in mustard plants. They were everywhere. It was almost surreal to see these plants flourishing right beside the highway in the dry and rocky soil where they are constantly saturated in exhaust fumes. These are definitely very tough plants. They possess a tenacious quality. You can plant mustard seeds in very rocky areas and because a mustard seed is so strong, when it begins to take root and then spring up it will quite literally push stones and "mountains" out of its way as it grows. It's no surprise that Jesus said that if our faith was *living* like a mustard seed that we, too, would move mountains.

How do we apply this teaching of Jesus to our lives today? What mountains do you have in your life that seem to be crushing you? What huge stone is sitting on you and crushing you or holding you back from doing what you know God has called you to do? Whatever it is, you can move it today. Whether it is spiritual forces, sickness, finances, or anything else, you can move it! Jesus says that these mountains will be removed. So take courage knowing that there is nothing in this life that can hold you back and keep you from victory. Today, in Jesus' name, you can move that mountain!

Chapter 3

At the Feast in Jerusalem

The Feast of Trumpets

In John 7 we read that Jesus attends the Feast of Booths or Tabernacles in Jerusalem. This celebration was preceded by the Feast of Trumpets or the Jewish New Year and then the Day of Atonement, which is covered in a later section of this chapter.

> The Lord said to Moses, "Say to the Israelites: 'On the first day of the seventh month you are to have a day of rest, a sacred assembly commemorated with trumpet blasts. Do no regular work, but present an offering made to the Lord by fire.'" (Lev. 23:23–25)

> On the first day of the seventh month hold a sacred assembly and do no regular work. It is a day for you to sound the trumpets. (Num. 29:1)

This feast takes place on the seventh month on the Jewish calendar, known as Tishri, and it was on this day God told Israel to celebrate this feast. The Feast of Trumpets is the one feast in which the simplest commands were given in respect to its requirements. He said, "Blow Trumpets." Such a simple command from the Lord, but yet this feast holds the greatest joy that a believer in Christ can hope for. This feast is a prophetic picture of the Rapture of the Bride of Christ.

Trumpets have a very significant role in Scripture. Let's look at a couple of verses in Scripture that deal with the blowing of trumpets. The first one is Matthew 24:31: "And he will send his angels with a loud trumpet call, and they will gather his elect from the four winds, from one end of the heavens to the other." Another is Joel 2:1: "Blow the trumpet in Zion; sound the alarm on my holy hill. Let all who live in the land tremble, for the day of the Lord is coming. It is close at hand."

Although it is called the Feast of Trumpets in Scripture, most people today would know it by its modern name, Rosh Hashanah. This phrase literally means "Head of the Year." Just like Passover begins the Jewish religious year, Trumpets begins the Jewish civil year. So in the Jewish community Rosh Hashanah is celebrated as the New Year. There are different reasons for this. Rabbinic tradition teaches that the world was created on Tishri 1, and some even teach that this was the very day on which man was created.[1]

During Bible times this feast was celebrated for only one day. However, as time went on, it was extended by the addition of a second day. The New Year is determined by the sighting of the new moon by two witnesses. To minimize the chance of an error in the sighting of the new moon and therefore celebrating the feast on the wrong date, the Jews added one day just to be safe. The Feast of Trumpets is the only feast for which no one really knows the day or hour when it will begin. They always know the season of Trumpets, but they can't pinpoint the day. It is possible this was the event that Jesus referred to in His comments about the end times in Matthew 24:36: "No one knows about that day or hour, not even the angels in heaven, nor the Son, but only the Father."[2]

It's interesting to note that it is necessary for two witnesses to come before the Feast of Trumpets can begin. In the Book of Revelation, John mentions that two witnesses will be sent by God in the last days. It is possible that these are the two witnesses who must come before the Rapture can take place. Consider the text and then we will consider the author and his culture. Revelation 11:3–4 states: "And I will give power to my two witnesses, and they will prophesy for 1,260 days, clothed in sackcloth. These are the two olive trees and the two lampstands that stand before the Lord of the earth." You have to remember that John was a Jewish male living within first-century Israel. The fact that he received the revelation while on the Island of Patmos has little or no bearing upon his theology. The prime influence upon his thinking and writing would be the Judaism of his day, which included many writings with powerful apocalyptic visions as well as the understanding of the feasts of the Lord. The idea of two witnesses coming before the Feast of Trumpets can begin is very much a first-century Jewish idea.

I am using the word "trumpet" quite a bit, but what do we mean when we say "trumpet"? Actually, the Hebrew word for "trumpet" is the word "shofar." The shofar is a ram's horn and was used at all the sacred gatherings of Israel and to make various pronouncements in the land.[3] Here are the many different purposes for blowing the trumpet in Bible times: to summon assemblies, to call together princes, to indicate when Israel should break camp and move on in the wilderness, and to sound an alarm. Trumpets were blown in times of war or enemy oppression but also used for days of gladness as well as solemn assemblies. They were blown at the beginning of each month and sounded during times of offerings and sacrifices. Trumpets were also used in the coronation ceremony of a new king. They were blown on the great day of the dedication of Solomon's Temple and for the great year of jubilee. As you can see, trumpets played a major role in ancient Israel.

Trumpets also play an important role when it comes to end-time events such as the Rapture of the church, the second coming of Christ, and God's final judgment. This feast takes place on the first day of the seventh month. In fact, all the prophetic feasts take place in the seventh month. It's interesting that God should choose the seventh month for the end-time feasts to be celebrated. It is clear in Scripture that the number 7 has a recurring role in God's end-time plans. In Scripture the number 7 represents completion and rest. It's no coincidence then that God should choose to place these feasts in the seventh month to represent the consummation of His plan in the end-time events.

Like all of Israel's feasts, this feast has natural as well as supernatural implications. Also, like so many of the other feasts, Rosh Hashanah has its own traditions and prophetic significance. The Feast of Trumpets is a time of reflection and forgiveness. This feast begins the season of what has come to be known as Israel's highest holy days of the year. The Feast of Trumpets is celebrated on the first day of Tishri and then the Day of Atonement (or Yom Kippur) is celebrated on the tenth day, where God will execute His judgment.

It's believed that the time between Trumpets and Atonement allows people the opportunity to seek forgiveness so that the Lord's wrath will pass over them. Literally, on the Day of Atonement God decides whether people will live or die that year as well as whether they will be blessed or not. So the days between Trumpets and Atonement are meant for making things right and for confession and restoration of relationships. As a result, these few days are the most important days on the Jewish calendar, both in biblical times as well as today.

According to Jewish tradition there are several things that happen during the Feast of Trumpets. Many other books discuss these traditions in detail. I mention them here in order to help us better understand the prophetic implications of Trumpets. The first tradition is that on the Day of Trumpets, God opens three books in heaven: the book of life for the wicked, the book of life for the righteous, and the book of life for those who are in between.[4]

I stated earlier that Trumpets marked the beginning of the high holy days, or what have also been called the days of awe. God opens up His books in heaven and waits to pronounce His judgment on the Day of Atonement. This might sound odd to us, but several Scriptures talk about different books being opened and names being either written or removed from their pages. Let's look at a few verses in both the Old and the New Testaments:

> May they be blotted out of the book of life and not be listed with the righteous. (Ps. 69:28)

> "But now, please forgive their sin—but if not, then blot me out of the book you have written." The Lord replied to Moses, "Whoever has sinned against me I will blot out of my book." (Exod. 32:32–33)

> He who overcomes will, like them, be dressed in white. I will never blot out his name from the book of life, but will acknowledge his name before my Father and his angels. (Rev. 3:5)

> And I saw the dead, great and small, standing before the throne, and books were opened. Another book was opened, which is the book of life. The dead were judged according to what they had done as recorded in the books. (Rev. 20:12)

These are but a few references to help us understand the thinking behind some of these ideas. So because it is believed that in this time period God writes or blots out the names of people from His book, tradition also teaches that it was during this feast that Satan would come to tempt people and lead them away from God so that their names would not go into the book of life. Jewish tradition teaches that the blast of the shofar confuses Satan, preventing him from bringing accusation against the people of God.[5] So it's no small wonder that today there are over one hundred shofar blasts during the Rosh Hashanah ceremony.[6] Keep in mind that these are *traditions* associated with the feasts and I am in no way implying that they are true, but rather, I only present them so that you will have a better understanding of the background of this feast.

Another tradition that is associated with this feast is what is known as the "Casting Ceremony." During this ceremony you go down to a stream or river and empty all of your pockets of bread crumbs and leaven. You are then to throw the bread into the water. The bread is symbolic of sin, and casting it into the water is symbolic of forgiveness. This ceremony has its roots in Micah 7:18–19: "Who is a God like you, who pardons sin and forgives the transgression of the remnant of his inheritance? You do not stay angry forever but delight to show mercy. You will again have compassion on us; you will tread our sins underfoot and hurl all our iniquities into the depths of the sea."

Another tradition of Rosh Hashanah is a rabbinical teaching regarding resurrection. Ancient Jewish theology teaches that the resurrection from the dead takes place on the first day of the Feast of Trumpets. The Scriptures are replete with references that link trumpet sounds to the concept of resurrection. This belief is not only ancient but modern as well. If you ever have a chance to walk through a Jewish cemetery you will find that many of the gravestones have pictures of shofars engraved on them, reflecting the belief that the departed one will be resurrected at the sound of the trumpet.[7]

This theology is also carried over into the New Testament. In fact, the Apostle Paul makes reference to this on more than one occasion. Paul's Jewishness is clearly illustrated in his doctrine concerning the resurrection. We need to remember that although the Apostle Paul was born in Tarsus, he received his advanced theological training in Jerusalem. As a Pharisee he was steeped in Jewish theology. He mentions this fact in Acts 23:6: "Then Paul, knowing that some of them were Sadducees and the others Pharisees, called out in the Sanhedrin, 'My brothers, I am a Pharisee, the son of a Pharisee. I stand on trial because of my hope in the resurrection of the dead.'"

Recently the church has begun to recognize and embrace the Jewishness of Jesus and to allow this knowledge to affect the way we see Jesus and His teachings. I would suggest that it is also very important for Christians to consider Paul in the same light. We must understand Paul's view of theology from a Hebrew perspective. Yes, Paul was the apostle to the Gentiles, but never forget who and what he was. In Philippians 3:3–6 he writes:

> For it is we who are the circumcision, we who worship by the Spirit of God, who glory in Christ Jesus, and who put no confidence in the flesh—though I myself have reasons for such confidence. If anyone else thinks he has reasons to put confidence in the flesh, I have more: circumcised on the eighth day, of the people of Israel, of the tribe of Benjamin, a Hebrew of Hebrews; in regard to the law, a Pharisee; as for zeal, persecuting the church; as for legalistic righteousness, faultless.

Consider Paul's teaching on the resurrection in 1 Corinthians 15:51–52: "Listen, I tell you a mystery: We will not all sleep, but we will all be changed—in a flash, in the twinkling of an eye, at the last trumpet. For the trumpet will sound, the dead will be raised imperishable, and we will be changed."

Again in 1 Thessalonians 4:13–18 we read:

> Brothers, we do not want you to be ignorant about those who fall asleep, or to grieve like the rest of men, who have no hope. We believe that Jesus died and rose again and so we believe that God will bring with Jesus those who have fallen asleep in him. According to the Lord's own word, we tell you that we who are still alive, who are left till the coming of the Lord, will certainly not precede those who have fallen asleep. For the Lord himself will come down from heaven, with a loud command, with the voice of the archangel and with the trumpet call of God, and the dead in Christ will rise first. After that, we who are still alive and are left will be caught up together with them in the clouds

> to meet the Lord in the air. And so we will be with the Lord forever. Therefore encourage each other with these words.

In this passage that describes the Rapture of the church, Paul's view of the resurrection is consistent with the Jewish perspective on resurrection. As we shall see, the Feast of Trumpets is, in fact, a beautiful prophetic picture of the Rapture of the Bride of Christ—the church. There has been much debate about this teaching, that the trumpet will sound and Christ will resurrect dead believers and catch away all living Christians to join Him for the great marriage supper of the Lamb in heaven. Some doubt the accuracy of this understanding while others hold various views concerning when it will take place. There are three distinct views in relation to the timing of the Rapture. Each one is in reference to the timing of the Tribulation period that precedes the Millennium. They are the Pre-Tribulation, Mid-Tribulation, and Post-Tribulation Rapture views.

The Pre-Tribulation view holds that the church will be raptured before the Tribulation period begins, the Mid-Tribulation view states that the church will be raptured halfway through the Tribulation, and the Post-Tribulation position holds that the church will have to endure the entire Tribulation and then be Raptured. It is not the purpose of this work to examine these different views. What I will do is present to you some parallels between the ancient Jewish wedding feast and some of the teaching that Jesus Himself gave concerning the end-times and allow you to come to your own decision.

The Bible speaks often of Jesus and His bride and in several cases we, the church, are directly called the Bride of Christ. Why that name for the church? Do Jesus and Paul simply use this language because it sounds nice, or is there a real purpose behind it? As we begin to understand the ancient Jewish betrothal and wedding practices, then the Scriptures regarding the end-times become clearer for us.

The people in Jesus' day knew exactly what He was going to do in the last days because they understood the principles of betrothal and marriage. It merits some exploration at least. Look at what Paul says in Ephesians 5:31–32: "For this reason a man will leave his father and mother and be united to his wife, and the two will become one flesh. This is a profound mystery—but I am talking about Christ and the church." It seems to be quite clear that Paul is directly linking the rituals of the ancient wedding ceremony to Christ and His church. Let's look at some of these practices. First we will see what the customs surrounding marriage in ancient Israel were and then we will see how Jesus has fulfilled and will fulfill the requirements of these customs.

The Marriage Covenant and the Bride Price

Today a man usually just asks for the bride's parents' blessing on his intention to marry their daughter and then they plan the wedding. In ancient Israel it was a much more involved process. When it came time for a man to marry he would first have to go to the young woman's house to present not only her but her father as well with a betrothal contract. This document clearly outlined to the young woman and her father how this young man was going to provide for his bride. He would state his occupation, salary, and living arrangements as well as his general plans and intentions for her.

The father would make the decision to accept or reject the man's offer. One of the most important issues surrounding the covenant was the bride price. How much was this young man willing to pay for this beautiful woman whom he wanted to marry? Not only would the bride price help compensate the family for the loss of their daughter, but more important, it demonstrated to the father how much the young man loved his daughter—the higher the price, the deeper the demonstration of his love for the girl.[8]

Keeping this first step of the betrothal process in mind, let's determine exactly how Jesus carried this out. At His final Passover supper with His disciples He accomplished the first requirement. He clearly stated to all those who were gathered how He was establishing a new covenant with them. He would provide for this covenant with the breaking of His body and by shedding His blood to fulfill the requirements necessary to keep the covenant.

In respect to the bride price He stated that He would pay for it with His life. Remember that the amount of the bride price determined the level of love.

How great was His love for us? Enough to give His life for us! As Peter wrote, "For you know that it was not with perishable things such as silver or gold that you were redeemed from the empty way of life handed down to you from your forefathers, but with the precious blood of Christ, a lamb without blemish or defect" (1 Pe. 1:18–19).

The Cup

The next step of betrothal involved the pouring and drinking from a cup. After the man's presentation of the betrothal contract he would pour a cup of wine and offer it to the woman. She would then drink of the cup. This indicated that she had accepted his proposal and the couple were then betrothed. This betrothal was legally binding and was the same as being married only without sexual consummation of the marriage. They could not refuse to marry unless they got a certificate of divorce. The man would then drink from the cup to indicate his joy that she had received him by receiving the cup.[9]

The couple would then separate and begin to make their preparations for the wedding day. They were not permitted to see each other during this process. The betrothal period would usually last between twelve and eighteen months.

Just as the bridegroom poured and offered a cup of wine to his bride, Jesus also offered a cup of wine to His disciples in the Upper Room on the night of His final Passover meal. Matthew 26:27–29 records: "Then he took the cup, gave thanks and offered it to them, saying, 'Drink from it, all of you. This is my blood of the covenant, which is poured out for many for the forgiveness of sins. I tell you, I will not drink of this fruit of the vine from now on until that day when I drink it anew with you in my Father's kingdom.'" He offered the cup to each of them and told them to drink. Each one there that night received the cup and therefore accepted the covenant Jesus was offering to them. At that point the Apostles, who form the foundation of the church, were betrothed to Christ.

Gifts for the Bride

After the acceptance of the contract the bridegroom would leave the woman with gifts. They were, first of all, a demonstration of his joy for her acceptance and, second, a sign of his affection for her. The gifts were also to serve as a reminder. He was about to go away for a long time and so the gifts were a reminder to her of him. Every time she would use one of the gifts that he had left for her, it would remind her of him and bring a smile to her face. So the purpose of these gifts was to keep the bride focused on her groom in his absence.[10]

Jesus also gave gifts to His bride, to us. Paul writes in Ephesians 4:7–8: "But to each one of us grace has been given as Christ apportioned it. This is why it says: 'When he ascended on high, he led captives in his train and gave gifts to men.'" Several of these gifts are listed in 1 Corinthians 12. It is extremely important for us to remember the purpose of the gifts. Jesus left us the gifts for one very specific reason: to remind us of Him. Every time you exercise one of the gifts that you have been given, it should bring all the attention and the glory to Christ.

Preparing a Place

After the contract had been established, the cup received, and the gifts given, it was time for the man to depart and go to prepare a place for his bride. The groom generally went back to his father's house to build an addition on the home where he and his bride would live.[11] The groom would spend the next couple of years preparing this new dwelling. It would be beautiful. After all, it was for the love of his life. Although the son would actually build the home, it was built according to the father's specifications. This was the place where the couple would come to spend their first seven days together (their honeymoon), so it was also called the wedding chamber.

Jesus also had to leave His newly betrothed bride to begin the next step of preparation. Remember that the son would go back to his father's house to begin constructing the new home. Jesus spoke about this in John 14:1–4: "Do not let your hearts be troubled. Trust in God; trust also in me. In my Father's house are many rooms; if it were not so, I would have told you. I am going there to prepare a place for you. And if I go and prepare a place for you, I will come back and take you to be with me that you also may be where I am. You know the way to the place where I am going." The parallel to the Jewish betrothal custom is obvious.

After the son went to his father's house and built the room where he and his bride would live, he had to wait until his father released him before he could go to claim his bride. If he was asked when he would receive his bride, he would have to say he did not know the day; only his father knew the time. Again let us look at Scripture for confirmation. Look at the following two verses in respect to this step in the process. The first is Mark 13:32. Jesus said, "No one knows about that day or hour, not even the angels in heaven, nor the Son, but only the Father." The second is Acts 1:6–7: "So when they met together, they asked him, 'Lord, are you at this time going to restore the kingdom to Israel?' He said to them: 'It is not for you to know the times or dates the Father has set by his own authority.'" Again, it seems very likely that Jesus had the betrothal process in mind.

A Waiting Bride

While the groom was away preparing the wedding chamber, the bride had a responsibility as well. Her job was to ready herself for his return. That's all she had to do. The contract had been established and accepted, so all she had to do was prepare herself for the day of his return. The bride was considered to be consecrated at this point. It was said of her that she had been bought with a price and was therefore set aside for the groom only. She would wear a veil over her head when she was out in public so that others would know she belonged only to her beloved. She would have saved all her money to use for her preparation period. She would not know the exact day or hour of his return, so she had to be ready at all times. Traditionally the groom would come at night and so she had to have her bags packed and lamps filled with oil ready by her bedside.[12]

As the Bride of Christ, we too are called to be consecrated or set apart for Him. Our task at this point is to prepare ourselves for His return. Sometimes the Church tends to get caught up in all sorts of things that cause divisions between believers. We must never lose sight of our focus, however, which is to be prepared for His return. It's interesting how the woman would save her money for the wedding. This money that she would bring to the groom was called her dowry. Without it she would not be able to marry. Also, the groom would give her money toward this dowry and she would dare not lose it. By keeping it safe and secure she showed her love for the groom.

Could it be that the woman who lost her coin in Luke 15 rejoiced when she found it because it was part of her dowry? In Luke 15:8–9 Jesus said, "Or suppose a woman has ten silver coins and loses one. Does she not light a lamp, sweep the house and search carefully until she finds it? And when she finds it, she calls her friends and neighbors together and says, 'Rejoice with me; I have found my lost coin.'"

The Coming of the Groom

The day would finally arrive when the father would release his son to go and get his bride. What an exciting day! Both the groom and the bride had been waiting with great anticipation for the hour to arrive. Usually in the evening the groomsmen would go ahead of him to the gate of the city where the bride lived. They would then sound the shofar to let her know that her groom had finally come. At the blast of the trumpet sound she would leave her home and come part of the way to the gate where the groom would be waiting for her. He would then take her away to the wedding chamber, where they would spend the next seven days together.[13]

Just as the groom would come in the middle of the night to steal his bride away at the sound of the shofar and she would meet him halfway, so, too, will Christ come for us and we shall rise to meet Him in the air. Paul makes reference to these betrothal practices in his first letter to the Thessalonians. In 1 Thessalonians 5:1–2 he writes: "Now, brothers, about times and dates we do not need to write to you, for you know very well that the day of the Lord will come like a thief in the night."

Paul then states in 1 Thessalonians 4:16-17: "For the Lord himself will come down from heaven, with a loud command, with the voice of the archangel and with the trumpet call of God, and the dead in Christ will rise first. After that, we who are still alive and are left will be caught up together with them in the clouds to meet the Lord in the air. And so we will be with the Lord forever."

It is very difficult to believe that the Apostle Paul did not have the betrothal process in mind when he penned those words under the inspiration of the Holy Spirit.

Seven Days in the Wedding Chamber

After he comes to take his bride away, the groom takes her back to his father's house, to what was called the wedding chamber.[14] This is where we get our modern version of the honeymoon. The couple would spend the next seven days together on their own. The members of the wedding party would wait for the seven days to be over and then come together again to hear the announcement that the marriage had been consummated. Then they would celebrate for seven days.

The Jews believed there would be a seven-year "time of trouble" that would come upon the earth. It was also known as the time of "Jacob's Trouble" or "The Birth Pains of the Messiah."[15] It was believed that the righteous would be resurrected just before this time and that they would enter the wedding chamber with the Messiah and be protected from this great and terrible time of trouble. Today in Christian circles we call this period of trouble the Great Tribulation.[16]

If we recognize how precisely Christ has fulfilled all but the last of the elements of the betrothal period, then it is with great confidence that we believe that He will fulfill the remaining prophetic requirement of the marriage contract. As the Bride of Christ, we will be "caught up" before the time of trouble and will spend that seven-year period in the wedding chamber in the Father's house. So we are called to await the return of our glorious Bridegroom as described in 1 Thessalonians 1:9–10. Here we learn that the Thessalonian believers had "turned to God from idols to serve the living and true God, and to wait for his Son from heaven, whom he raised from the dead—Jesus, who rescues us from the coming wrath."

Departure for Their New Home

After the wedding celebration, the bride and the groom would depart for their new home that the groom had prepared for them. Even to this day, if you go to Israel you will see beautifully built houses with unfinished exposed rooms in the house, usually on the second floor or on an adjoining part of the property. If you ask the father of the home why he has these unfinished rooms, he will tell you that they are for his sons so that when each gets married he will have a place to come back to and build a wedding chamber for his bride.

Just as the bride and bridegroom would emerge and return to their new home, so, too, will we return with Christ to our new home that He has prepared for us:

> Then I saw a new heaven and a new earth, for the first heaven and the first earth had passed away, and there was no longer any sea. I saw the Holy City, the new Jerusalem, coming down out of heaven from God,

prepared as a bride beautifully dressed for her husband. And I heard a loud voice from the throne saying, "Now the dwelling of God is with men, and he will live with them. They will be his people, and God himself will be with them and be their God. He will wipe every tear from their eyes. There will be no more death or mourning or crying or pain, for the old order of things has passed away." He who was seated on the throne said, "I am making everything new!" Then he said, "Write this down, for these words are trustworthy and true." He said to me: "It is done. I am the Alpha and the Omega, the Beginning and the End. To him who is thirsty I will give to drink without cost from the spring of the water of life. He who overcomes will inherit all this, and I will be his God and he will be my son. But the cowardly, the unbelieving, the vile, the murderers, the sexually immoral, those who practice magic arts, the idolaters and all liars—their place will be in the fiery lake of burning sulfur. This is the second death." One of the seven angels who had the seven bowls full of the seven last plagues came and said to me, "Come, I will show you the bride, the wife of the Lamb." And he carried me away in the Spirit to a mountain great and high, and showed me the Holy City, Jerusalem, coming down out of heaven from God. (Rev. 21:1–10)

Conclusion

I began this section by looking at the Feast of Trumpets and noted how this is connected prophetically to the return of Christ. I then reviewed the Jewish wedding customs and noted how intricately they correspond to the events surrounding Christ's return for His Bride, the church. We can see Jesus had these ancient Jewish customs in mind when He spoke of His return. Once we begin to view the words and deeds of Jesus in their original cultural context, we have fresh insight into the meaning and significance of His teachings. May we all be ready and waiting for the great trumpet of the Lord to sound on that day.

The Day of Atonement

The Day of Atonement comes eight days after Trumpets and five days before Tabernacles. This feast is described in Leviticus 16 and 23:

> "This is to be a lasting ordinance for you: On the tenth day of the seventh month you must deny yourselves and not do any work—whether native-born or an alien living among you—because on this day atonement will be made for you, to cleanse you. Then, before the Lord, you will be clean from all your sins. It is a Sabbath of rest, and you must deny yourselves; it is a lasting ordinance. The priest who is anointed and ordained to succeed his father as high priest is to make atonement. He is to put on the sacred linen garments and make atonement for the Most Holy Place, for the Tent of Meeting and the altar, and for the priests and

> all the people of the community. This is to be a lasting ordinance for you: Atonement is to be made once a year for all the sins of the Israelites." And it was done, as the Lord commanded Moses. (Lev. 16:29–34)

> The tenth day of this seventh month is the Day of Atonement. Hold a sacred assembly and deny yourselves, and present an offering made to the Lord by fire. Do no work on that day, because it is the Day of Atonement, when atonement is made for you before the Lord your God. Anyone who does not deny himself on that day must be cut off from his people. I will destroy from among his people anyone who does any work on that day. You shall do no work at all. This is to be a lasting ordinance for the generations to come, wherever you live. It is a Sabbath of rest for you, and you must deny yourselves. From the evening of the ninth day of the month until the following evening you are to observe your Sabbath. (Lev. 23:27–32)

The Day of Atonement takes place on Tishri 10. It was and still is Israel's most holy day. We saw how the Feast of Trumpets was a picture of the Rapture of the church. The Day of Atonement is also filled with prophetic imagery. In the section dealing with the Feast of Firstfruits in chapter 6 I will identify the Messianic role of the High Priest. There are also Messianic implications related to the Day of Atonement Feast.

The Day of Atonement speaks of the judgment of God.[17] In modern Judaism, it is believed that this is the day when God makes His judgment that will affect your life for the upcoming year. During Trumpets, the message was all about forgiveness and repentance. During Atonement, the message is judgment. While all the other holidays are feasts, the Day of Atonement is actually a fast. Because of the magnitude of the message of this holiday, it stands alone above all the rest.

This biblical holiday is also known as "Yom Kippur." "Yom Kippur" translated into English simply means "The Day of Atonement." This is the sixth holiday on God's prophetic calendar, and it takes place during the seventh month. It's important to note at this time that all of the fall feasts take place during this month. We must remember that the number 7 represents completion or perfection. So with this in mind, we can see why God chose this month for these feasts to occur, because they complete God's plan for mankind.

While I've already discussed how important this day was for the people, we also need to remember what an important day it was for the High Priest of Israel. While the entire nation awaited God's decision for the future, the High Priest was preparing himself for the most important day of the year. This was the only day he was allowed to enter the Holy of Holies. On no other day could he come that close to God's presence. If he was to enter the Holy of Holies at any other time, he would surely die. Yet on this incredible day he could come into the presence of Almighty God and offer sacrifices on behalf of the people to atone for their sins.

It's also good to mention at this point that the sacrifices offered on this day had to be repeated on an annual basis. The people looked forward to the day when God would send His Lamb, not to cover up their sins for another year but to remove the stain of sin once and for all. After the High Priest made all of the required sacrifices for the Feast of Trumpets, he was to go into seclusion for seven days to avoid becoming defiled for his duties on the Day of Atonement.[18]

The first sacrifice is a sin offering of a bullock for the High Priest and his family. The next sacrifice was for the people of Israel. There was a ceremony that involved two goats. The goats were brought in before the High Priest and lots were cast to decide the order of the sacrifice of each goat (Lev. 16:6–9). The golden lots had inscriptions on them. One said: "For Adonai" (the Lord) and the other was marked: "For Azazel." There have been different interpretations for the meaning of "Azazel," but it's generally agreed that it is a reference to Satan.[19] The goat on which the lot of Adonai fell was immediately sacrificed on behalf of the people. The goat on which the lot of Azazel fell was marked with a scarlet strip of wool that was tied around its horns.

At this point the High Priest would place his hands upon the head of the goat marked for Azazel and symbolically transfer the sins of the people to the goat. Following this, the goat was then released into the wilderness, thus carrying away the sins of the people (Lev. 16:20–22). This ancient practice gives us our modern term "scapegoat," referring to one who is chosen to accept the blame of others. It's interesting that the goat was released into the desert and not into any other place. In ancient Israel, it was believed by the people that the desert was inhabited by demons and even Satan himself. Compare this with the fact that Jesus went into the desert to be tempted by Satan after His baptism by John.

Initially the goat was released into the desert. This practice was later revised because occasionally the goat would wander into a neighboring town or city. In order to prevent this from happening, the rabbis introduced another practice into the Yom Kippur tradition. Instead of releasing the goat into the desert, they actually brought the goat to the edge of a cliff and threw it off the cliff backward to ensure the act was complete. Before the priest would push the goat backward, he would tear off a portion of the scarlet strip of wool that was tied around one of its horns.[20] Ancient Jewish literature records a most phenomenal event. It was said that the piece of scarlet wool that the priest held in his hand would turn white as the goat fell.[21] This was a sign to the people that their sins had in fact been forgiven and removed for another year. Consider the similarity of this concept with what is written in Isaiah 1:18: "'Come now, let us reason together,' says the Lord. 'Though your sins are like scarlet, they shall be as white as snow; though they are red as crimson, they shall be like wool.'"

This practice was carried on for hundreds of years by the priests and brought great comfort and solace to the people. They knew every year that God would forgive their sins. Every year, as the scarlet wool turned white, they would take comfort in knowing that as long as the priest performed his duty in the proper manner, their sins would be cleansed for another year. Amazingly, ancient Jewish literature records that the scarlet piece of wool stopped turning white after the death and resurrection of Jesus.[22] Can we consider this coincidence or divine design?

We know now that it is not by the blood of goats that we have forgiveness of sins because Christ—Who is God's Passover Lamb—has been slain for us. In ancient days, the blood of goats only covered the sins of the people and had to be repeated year after year, but Christ died once for all. The Bible speaks clearly about this in Hebrews 10:1–14:

> The law is only a shadow of the good things that are coming—not the realities themselves. For this reason it can never, by the same sacrifices repeated endlessly year after year, make perfect those who draw near to worship. If it could, would they not have stopped being offered? For the worshipers would have been cleansed once for all, and would no longer have felt guilty for their sins. But those sacrifices are an annual reminder of sins, because it is impossible for the blood of bulls and goats to take away sins.
>
> Therefore, when Christ came into the world, he said: "Sacrifice and offering you did not desire, but a body you prepared for me; with burnt offerings and sin offerings you were not pleased." Then I said, "Here I am—it is written about me in the scroll—I have come

> to do your will, O God." First he said, "Sacrifices and offerings, burnt offerings and sin offerings you did not desire, nor were you pleased with them" (although the law required them to be made). Then he said, "Here I am, I have come to do your will." He sets aside the first to establish the second. And by that will, we have been made holy through the sacrifice of the body of Jesus Christ once for all.
>
> Day after day every priest stands and performs his religious duties; again and again he offers the same sacrifices, which can never take away sins. But when this priest had offered for all time one sacrifice for sins, he sat down at the right hand of God. Since that time he waits for his enemies to be made his footstool, because by one sacrifice he has made perfect forever those who are being made holy.

Thus the sacrifice of Christ provides the one and only way for all humankind to receive the full and final forgiveness of sins. No more do the sacrifices have to be made year after year. Instead we can celebrate freedom from sin's guilt and power through the precious blood of Jesus!

The Feast of Tabernacles

John describes how Jesus went up to the feasts privately in order to avoid confrontation with the authorities until the time was right. Then in the middle of the

Feast of Tabernacles, He begins to teach in the Temple (John 7:1–14). The requirements for this feast are described in Leviticus 23 and Deuteronomy 16:

> Say to the Israelites: "On the fifteenth day of the seventh month the Lord's Feast of Tabernacles begins, and it lasts for seven days." (Lev. 23:34)

> Celebrate the Feast of Tabernacles for seven days after you have gathered the produce of your threshing floor and your winepress. Be joyful at your Feast—you, your sons and daughters, your menservants and maidservants, and the Levites, the aliens, the fatherless and the widows who live in your towns. For seven days celebrate the Feast to the Lord your God at the place the Lord will choose. For the Lord your God will bless you in all your harvest and in all the work of your hands, and your joy will be complete. Three times a year all your men must appear before the Lord your God at the place he will choose: at the Feast of Unleavened Bread, the Feast of Weeks and the Feast of Tabernacles. No man should appear before the Lord empty-handed. (Deut. 16:13–16)

The Feast of Tabernacles takes place on the fifteenth day of the seventh month and is an annual reminder of Israel's forty-year wandering in the desert. There are various names by which this feast is called. Its most common name is the one that we've already used, which is the Feast of Tabernacles. It is also referred to as the Feast of Booths and by its Hebrew name,

Sukkot. There are three basic aspects to this feast—it speaks to us in terms of God's past, present, and future activity within mankind.

The Feast of Tabernacles reminds us of God's supernatural intervention during the freeing of the Israelites from Egyptian bondage. We are reminded of God's display of power as He led them through the Red Sea. We see how He provided for their every need as He took them from the land of slavery into the Promised Land. Every year it reminds us of how God rained down manna each day and how He caused water to come out of a rock to quench the thirst of an entire nation. The Feast of Tabernacles also reminds us of God's ever-present nature. We remember how God directed His people with a cloud by day and with a pillar of fire by night. As they journeyed through the wilderness, they dwelt in temporary dwellings called *sukkah*. For forty years, God faithfully protected and provided for His children.

Today the Feast of Tabernacles falls during the time of the final harvest in Israel and it occurs just before the rainy season. It's a season of thanksgiving and rejoicing because of God's provision of the crops that year. God commanded that the people were to dwell in tabernacles for seven days. Today we can see this feast as a time to separate ourselves from the comforts of life in order for us to identify with what the Israelites endured. As we live in the tabernacles, we are brought to a level of simplicity that helps free us from our slavery to materialism. As we dwell in the tabernacles, we are reminded of the fact that God and not our possessions is the source of our joy. We remember that there is protection and safety in the covering of our God. We know that because He has provided He will continue to provide.

Not only does the Feast of Tabernacles speak of God's activity in the past and in the present, but it also speaks of a time when God will once again intervene directly in the affairs of humanity. We look forward with great anticipation to the day when, once again, God will "tabernacle" with man in the fullest measure possible. As it was in the beginning when God and man enjoyed fellowship face-to-face, so shall it be in the end. Revelation 21:1–3 paints a beautiful picture for us of our glorious future:

> Then I saw a new heaven and a new earth, for the first heaven and the first earth had passed away, and there was no longer any sea. I saw the Holy City, the New Jerusalem, coming down out of heaven from God, prepared as a bride beautifully dressed for her husband. And I heard a loud voice from the throne saying, "Now the dwelling of God is with men, and he will live with them. They will be his people, and God himself will be with them and be their God."

There are three distinct areas in relation to this feast that I want to deal with in this section. The first area is in regards to a tradition that evolved during the First Temple period, which was the time of Solomon's Temple. King Solomon dedicated the Temple to the Lord during the Feast of Tabernacles (2 Chron. 7:1–10). The

Bible records an extraordinary event that took place during the dedication.

After Solomon prayed and dedicated the Temple, the Shekinah glory of God fell from heaven and filled the Temple. Jewish tradition says that the fire actually lit the altar and the candles within the Holy of Holies. Because of this event, the people associated the Feast of Tabernacles with the return of the glory of God to the Temple. We read about it in 2 Chronicles 7:1–3:

> When Solomon finished praying, fire came down from heaven and consumed the burnt offering and the sacrifices, and the glory of the Lord filled the temple. The priests could not enter the temple of the Lord because the glory of the Lord filled it. When all the Israelites saw the fire coming down and the glory of the Lord above the temple, they knelt on the pavement with their faces to the ground, and they worshiped and gave thanks to the Lord, saying, "He is good; his love endures forever."

In the light of this association between the Feast of Tabernacles and the return of the glory of God to the Temple, the accounts in the Gospel of John take on a new and powerful significance. Before we read the Scripture, let's go over in our minds what people were expecting during this feast. The glory of God filled the Temple on the last and greatest day of the Feast of Tabernacles. So, year after year, people anticipated the return of God's glory to the Temple on this specific day.

The disciple John records for us in his Gospel the activity of Jesus during this feast. It's important for us to remember that John was a first-century Jew writing to first-century Jews who knew and expected certain things to happen. We have to remember to pay attention to the details of Scripture. Events and details have not been placed there by chance. They are placed there because John wants to take his readers to a revelational discovery. This is what he writes in John 7:37: "On the last and greatest day of the Feast, Jesus stood and said in a loud voice, 'If anyone is thirsty, let him come to me and drink.'"

What day does John record that Jesus cried out in the Temple? It was "the last and greatest day of the Feast" of Tabernacles. Why is this important? It is important because the people expected the glory of God to manifest itself in the Temple on that specific day. Simply put, the mere presence of Jesus in the Temple that day represented one of His greatest Messianic claims. Jesus coming to the Temple on that specific day was God's way of saying to the people that His glory, in the person of His Son, had returned to the Temple.

Another tradition associated with the Feast of Tabernacles is what is called the water libation ceremony.[23] It was a visual prayer for rain. Israel has always depended on the fall rains in order for the harvest to ripen. Rain has always been a symbol of life to the Jewish people. During this ceremony, several steps were taken in order to ensure that God would once again send the rains the land so desperately needed. The High Priest would exit the Temple and begin to descend down the side of the Temple Mount and make his way to the Pool of Siloam, which was filled with living water, that is, water that was spring fed and therefore constantly moving. The High Priest would carry two golden pitchers with him, and when he arrived at the pool he would then dip and fill both pitchers with the living water. The procession would then leave the pool and make their way back to the Temple. Once the High Priest reached the altar, he would then begin to pour the living water over the altar.[24] This ceremony was performed on each day of the feast. It was a prayer for God to send the living water and on the last day it would release faith in the people to believe that God would send them His living water that day.

Picture in your mind this libation ceremony taking place in the light of John 7:37–38, where Jesus makes His Messianic claim. It says: "On the last and greatest day of the Feast, Jesus stood and said in a loud voice, 'If anyone is thirsty, let him come to me and drink. Whoever believes in me, as the Scripture has said, streams of living water will flow from within him.'" By saying this, Jesus was implying that He was the Living Water sent from God That they were praying for. By understanding the events that were taking place when Jesus made this statement, we see that it adds greater depth and significance to His words that day.

Ancient Jewish literature records for us another custom that developed over time, which was practiced in the time of Christ during the Feast of Tabernacles, called the Illumination of the Temple Ceremony.[25]

There were four large menorahs or candelabra in the Temple courtyard. Some literature suggests that these menorahs were a staggering seventy feet tall. In any event, we know that they were very large. During each day of the feast, these menorahs were lit in an area of the Temple known as the Women's Court. It was said that they cast such a bright light that they illuminated every courtyard in Jerusalem. Once again, with this ceremony in the forefront of our minds, we come to the statement of Jesus in John 8:12: "When Jesus spoke again to the people, he said, 'I am the light of the world. Whoever follows me will never walk in darkness, but will have the light of life.'" When He made this statement, both the people and the priests knew exactly what Jesus was referring to. For six nights they saw the blazing light of the menorahs in the Temple courts.

Shortly after leaving the Temple, Jesus reinforced His statements, as He often did, with actions. He did not just claim to be the Light of the World; He displayed powerfully that He was, in fact, what and who He said He was. After he had made the claim, "I am the light of the world," in the Temple courts, he went on to prove it by healing a man who was born blind. The story is found in John 9:1–7:

> As he went along, he saw a man blind from birth. His disciples asked him, "Rabbi, who sinned, this man or his parents, that he was born blind?" "Neither this man nor his parents sinned," said Jesus, "but this happened so that the work of God might be displayed in

> his life. As long as it is day, we must do the work of him who sent me. Night is coming, when no one can work. While I am in the world, I am the light of the world." Having said this, he spit on the ground, made some mud with the saliva, and put it on the man's eyes. "Go," he told him, "wash in the Pool of Siloam" [this word means "sent"]. So the man went and washed, and came home seeing.

The most powerful message of the Feast of Tabernacles is the fact of God's desire to have intimate fellowship with His creation. Since sin first entered the world, it has been God's desire to have our relationship with Him restored. We know that Christ has reconciled man unto God. In and through Jesus's birth, life, and death, God has made His dwelling with man. Not only was Jesus the Tabernacle of God, but He also came to tabernacle with man as found in John 1:14: "And the Word (Christ) became flesh (human, incarnate) and tabernacled (fixed His tent of flesh, lived awhile) among us; and we [actually] saw His glory (His honor, His majesty), such glory as an only begotten son receives from his father, full of grace (favor, loving-kindness) and truth" (AMP).

Writing in the Sand

On the last day of the Feast of Tabernacles, Jesus cries out in the Temple, "If anyone is thirsty, let him come to Me and drink" (John 7:37). Following this there is discussion among the people as to who He might be. Jesus spends the night on the Mount of Olives and returns the next morning to the Temple, where He is confronted by the authorities trying to trap Him into denying the Law. John describes their attempt:

> The teachers of the Law and the Pharisees brought in a woman caught in adultery. They made her stand before the group and said to Jesus, "Teacher, this woman was caught in the act of adultery. In the Law Moses commanded us to stone such women. Now what do you say?" They were using this question as a trap, in order to have a basis for accusing him. But Jesus bent down and started to write on the ground with his finger.
>
> When they kept on questioning him, he straightened up and said to them, "If any one of you is without sin, let him be the first to throw a stone at her." Again he stooped down and wrote on the ground. At this, those who heard began to go away one at a time, the older ones first, until only Jesus was left, with the woman still standing there. Jesus straightened up and asked her, "Woman, where are they? Has no one condemned you?" "No one, sir," she said. "Then neither do I condemn you," Jesus declared. "Go now and leave your life of sin." (John 8:3–11)

We are all familiar with this passage of Scripture. I'm sure we all share a common question surrounding this story: What did Jesus write in the sand? In order to understand the events surrounding this story fully, there are two fundamental questions we need to address: When and where did the story take place?

Let's first address the "where" question. The text says that the teachers of the Law brought an adulterous woman before Him. This event could only have occurred in one location in the Temple area and that would be the Outer Court (also known as the Women's Court or the Gentiles' Court). This was an area on the Temple Mount where there were no limitations on who could be there. Beyond the Outer Court was an area of the Temple known as the Holy Place, and in this area only righteous men were permitted to enter with their sacrifices. Beyond the Holy Place was the Holy of Holies, the sacred chamber where the Glory of God dwelled, and in this area only the High Priest on one day of the year was granted access. Here we see a pattern in the layout of the Temple—the closer we want to get to God's presence, the more holiness is required of us.

Now that we've established the "where" question, we'll look at the "when" of this event. To pinpoint the day, we need to look back a few hours to what led up to the story we're examining. Prior to this event, John 7:37–44 records:

> On the last and greatest day of the Feast, Jesus stood (in the temple) and said in a loud voice, "If anyone is thirsty, let him come to me and drink. Whoever believes in me, as the Scripture has said, streams of living water will flow from within him." By this he meant the

> Spirit, whom those who believed in him were later to receive. Up to that time the Spirit had not been given, since Jesus had not yet been glorified.
>
> On hearing his words, some of the people said, "Surely this man is the Prophet." Others said, "He is the Christ." Still others asked, "How can the Christ come from Galilee? Does not the Scripture say that the Christ will come from David's family and from Bethlehem, the town where David lived?" Thus the people were divided because of Jesus. Some wanted to seize him, but no one laid a hand on him.

Some people wanted to accept Jesus as the Messiah, and others rejected Him as their Messiah.

John is very specific in mentioning that this encounter with the Pharisees and the adulterous woman took place on the very next day following the last and greatest day of the feast. As we have learned in the last section, during the Second Temple era there was a ceremony associated with the Feast of Tabernacles known as the water libation ceremony. This ceremony took place in the Temple every day during the feast and culminated in a glorious worship service on the last day. As we have seen, it was during this water ceremony on the last day of the feast that Jesus cried out, "If anyone is thirsty, let him come to me and drink. Whoever believes in me, as the Scripture has said, streams of living water will flow from within him" (John 7:37–38). This was a bold and unequivocal statement of His Messiahship to Israel.

In the verses that follow, John describes the sharp

disagreement that erupted over this claim among those who were in the Temple area. While some accepted Jesus' claims, others rejected them. The following day the teachers of the Law bring the accused woman to Him for His interpretation of what the Law had to say about her sin. Here we see a prime example of the Remez method in action (see "First-Century Idioms" in the introduction). Instead of coming right out and verbalizing His thoughts, He stoops down and writes in the sand. Notice that the accusers do not respond to this but continue to question Him. Then Jesus plainly asks for the one without sin to cast the first stone. Jesus is focusing on the issue of personal sin, not only that of the woman but that of her accusers as well.

There is no response to the first time Jesus writes in the sand, nor to his direct addressing of their sin, so He continues to write in the sand. This brings an unexpected response. The accusers drop their stones one by one and walk away! What did Jesus write that caused the woman's accusers to leave?

Keeping in mind the issue of personal sin and the rejection of Jesus as God's Living Water, let's look at a passage found in Jeremiah 17:13: "O Lord, the hope of Israel, all who forsake you will be put to shame. Those who turn away from you will be written in the dust because they have forsaken the Lord, the spring of living water." Wow! What a passage! It bears a striking resemblance to this story of Jesus' encounter with the adulterous woman and the Pharisees. Jesus is again using the Remez method of dropping hints that point the accusers to this portion of Scripture. The text says that those who turn away from the Lord (sinners) will have their names written in the dust because they have rejected God's Living Water.

At the time when the people are asking God to give them living water, Jesus claims to be the Living Water they have been waiting, longing, and searching for. He is then rejected by them and writes their names in the dust. It is no surprise that the accusers dropped their stones and left. As they were teachers very well versed in the Torah, their thoughts would have undoubtedly gone to the passage in Jeremiah and they would have made the logical connection between the prophecy and the actions of Jesus.

The Third Messianic Miracle—Healing a Man Born Blind

Following the confrontation over the woman caught in adultery, Jesus teaches in the Temple about His relationship to the Father and then leaves as some pick up stones to stone Him (John 8:12–59). Possibly on His way out of the Temple, or shortly thereafter, He encounters a blind man.

The following passage records for us the third Messianic miracle of Jesus:

> As he went along, he saw a man blind from birth. His disciples asked him, "Rabbi, who sinned, this man or his parents, that he was born blind?" "Neither this

> man nor his parents sinned," said Jesus, "but this happened so that the work of God might be displayed in his life.
>
> "As long as it is day, we must do the work of him who sent me. Night is coming, when no one can work. While I am in the world, I am the light of the world." Having said this, he spit on the ground, made some mud with the saliva, and put it on the man's eyes. "Go," he told him, "wash in the Pool of Siloam." So the man went and washed, and came home seeing. (John 9:1–7)

This is another powerful Messianic miracle of Jesus. Others who came before Jesus made a lot of claims and said a lot of things, but Jesus backed up His claims with actions. In this passage He tells his disciples He is the Light of the world and then He proves it by healing a man born blind.

In the days of Jesus, Jews believed that only the Messiah would be able to heal a man who was blind from birth. Blindness was said to be a curse from God, and therefore only God could remove that curse. So when Jesus performed this miracle it definitely got the attention of the people—especially the Pharisees.

Following his healing the blind man then begins walking around town. Some of his neighbors and those who have seen him begging start to recognize him as the man who was born blind, but others say it is not him. Then the man himself confirms it by saying, "I am the one" (John 9:9). They demand to know who healed him. He describes how Jesus anointed his eyes and sent him to the Pool of Siloam to wash. When the neighbors hear this they take him to the Pharisees to be interrogated because it was on the Sabbath that he was healed. The Pharisees ask how he was healed and the man recounts the story. They reject his account and go on to suggest that he is lying about being born blind, so they call for his parents to verify the information. His parents arrive and the Pharisees question them. They confirm to the Pharisees that this is, in fact, their son and that he was born blind.

After hearing all this evidence, the Pharisees ask the man again to tell them who healed him and how. In frustration he suggests that perhaps they are asking him again because they want to become disciples of Jesus. The Pharisees quickly respond by saying that they are followers of Moses, because he was a righteous man. The formerly blind man then argues that if Jesus was a sinner, then how could God use Him to perform a miracle? Then the blind man puts the icing on the cake. Consider what he says in John 9:32: "Nobody has ever heard of opening the eyes of a man born blind."

No matter how they try to get around it, the Pharisees cannot deny that Jesus has performed a miracle they believed only God could do, one that Jewish tradition claimed could only be done by the Messiah.

Chapter 4

The Ministry in Judea

The Feast of Dedication

At some point following the Feast of Tabernacles, Jesus is again in Jerusalem during the time of the Feast of Dedication that takes place in November or December depending on the year. We read about it in John 10:22: "Then came the Feast of Dedication at Jerusalem. It was winter." The Message translation puts it this way: "They were celebrating Hanukkah just then in Jerusalem. It was winter" (John 10:22).

Few believers have recognized the significance of this event due to a lack of understanding regarding the feasts in general and this one in particular. The New International Version calls it the Feast of Dedication, as do most versions. The Message version uses the modern name for this celebration: Hanukkah. This feast is rarely discussed in the church. The assumption is that it is a Jewish holiday and therefore belongs to the Jewish people.

It has already been stressed that we need to understand that the feasts were a very important part of Jesus' life. We shouldn't be surprised to find Him in Jerusalem celebrating Hanukkah. Keep in mind that Christmas and Easter were instituted by the church hundreds of years after the life, death, and resurrection of Jesus. We also know that in the beginning the early church continued to celebrate the Jewish feasts and festivals. The story and the message behind Hanukkah are powerful ones.

Hanukkah is also known as the Festival of Lights. It is an eight-day holiday that commemorates the rededication of the Temple in Jerusalem. It begins on the twenty-fifth day of Kislev according to the Hebrew calendar, which generally coincides with late November or early December on our calendar. Many people wonder how this festival got started, since it was not included among the original feasts that God gave in the Torah.

In 167 BC Antiochus IV, the ruler of Syria, had moved his forces into Jerusalem and had taken over the Temple. He ordered that an altar to Zeus be built in the Holy Temple. While this outraged the Jewish people, it was the desecration of the Temple by the offering of a pig on the altar of sacrifice that was the proverbial last straw for the people. They had tolerated much under Antiochus, but this time he had gone too far.[1]

In 165 BC, in response to this abomination, a group known as the Maccabees revolted and miraculously recaptured the Temple of the Lord. In the Temple there was a menorah—also known as the eternal flame—which was to burn continuously. On the day the Maccabees took back the Temple there was only enough consecrated olive oil to keep the menorah lit for one day. Despite this, the menorah kept burning for eight days, the exact amount of time it took to press, prepare, and consecrate fresh olive oil. It was a miracle! In response to this miracle the Maccabees and the entire congregation of Israel decided that the time of rededicating the Temple should be celebrated every year for eight days.

Today this feast is celebrated in Jewish homes by the lighting of eight successive candles on a special Hanukkah menorah. There are actually nine candles on the menorah. The center one is used to light the rest. On each night of Hanukkah, one more candle is lit. On the first night, only one candle is lit. On the second night two candles are lit, and so forth. What is the meaning of Hanukkah and how can it be applied to believers today? In the days of the Temple, the people gave God what they had, which was enough oil for only one day. God honored that gift and put His "super" on their "natural" and the flame burned for eight days.

The lesson for us is simple: Give God what you have, no matter how small or insignificant you may think it is. In the hands of God, your gifts and talents can be transformed into a powerful tool. Wouldn't it be great for us as believers to take time during Hanukkah to reflect on the gifts that God has given us and prayerfully consider how we can use them to the glory of God—to give God whatever we have, no matter how small, and watch what He will do with it?

The Cost of Discipleship

After the Feast of Dedication Jesus spends some time on the other side of the Jordan and eventually returns to Galilee. Later He leaves Galilee headed for Judea. He has just passed through a Samaritan village where He was turned away. Someone offers to follow Him, which leads Jesus into a teaching on the cost of discipleship. Matthew records a remark by a second would-be disciple: "Another disciple said to him, 'Lord, first let me go and bury my father.' But Jesus told him, 'Follow me, and let the dead bury their own dead'" (Matt. 8:21–22).

Without proper understanding of cultural practices during the time of Jesus, the statement Jesus made to this disciple sounds very harsh. It also gives the impression that He is telling this disciple to break the fifth commandment found in Exodus 20:12: "Honor your father and your mother, so that you may live long in the land the Lord your God is giving you."

Do you really think that Jesus, being the very form of God Himself, would tell a disciple to desecrate the very commandment He gave? I don't think so. In order to understand the real meaning behind the seemingly harsh remark, we must understand the burial traditions that were observed by those living in Israel in the first century.

These traditions required that the body of the deceased be buried the same day. This is in accordance with Deuteronomy 21:22–23: "If a man guilty of a capital offense is put to death and his body is hung on a tree, you must not leave his body on the tree overnight. Be sure to bury him that same day, because anyone who is hung on a tree is under God's curse. You must not desecrate the land the Lord your God is giving you as an inheritance."

Another passage that shows this principle in practice is in the story of Ananias and Sapphira found in Acts 5:5–10:

> When Ananias heard this, he fell down and died. And great fear seized all who heard what had happened. Then the young men came forward, wrapped up his body, and carried him out and buried him. About three hours later his wife came in, not knowing what had happened. Peter asked her, "Tell me, is this the price you and Ananias got for the land?" "Yes,' she said, "that is the price." Peter said to her, "How could you agree to test the Spirit of the Lord? Look! The feet of the men who buried your husband are at the door, and they will carry you out also." At that moment she fell down at his feet and died. Then the young men came in and, finding her dead, carried her out and buried her beside her husband.

You will notice in both of these passages that the body was buried the same day. This was called the first burial. After this, the family was to observe a seven-day period of mourning called shiva. During this special mourning period they were not even permitted to leave the house.

The body was then placed in a burial chamber where it was left to decompose. The Jerusalem Talmud says: "When the flesh had wasted away, the bones were collected and placed in small chests called ossuaries. After the flesh had gone from the bones, and the bones were placed in the ossuaries, the son stopped mourning."[2]

The transfer of the bones to the ossuary was called the second burial. What would happen is that the oldest son would take the bones of his father to either the Holy City of Jerusalem or to the family burial cave, where they were deposited with the bones of their ancestors. The Jews believed that during the time required for the decomposition of the flesh between the first and second burial, atonement was achieved for the person.[3] It was only after the sinful flesh was off the bones that the sins could be atoned for. Although this second burial tradition and the beliefs concerning atonement associated with it did not have a scriptural basis, it had become common practice by the time of Jesus.

So, as we can see, Jesus was in no way hindering the disciple from keeping the fifth commandment by telling him not to bury his father. Instead, Jesus was denying the validity of the second burial tradition, both because it was given by man and not by God and because it suggested falsely that anything other than the Messiah could deliver a person from sin.[4]

Some have used this passage to suggest that Jesus was saying that ministry comes before family. Some have even gone so far as to say that family must never come before ministry—that it is a sin. In light of our understanding of this passage in its cultural context, that type of thinking could not be further from the truth.

The Camel and the Eye of the Needle

Following a lengthy section recorded only by Luke (9:51–18:14), Jesus is coming to Jerusalem for the last time. Along the way Jesus encounters a rich young man who wants to follow Him. The young man asks, "Teacher, what good thing must I do to get eternal life?" Jesus tells him to keep the commandments. He replies, "All these I have kept. What do I still lack?" Jesus tells him to sell his possessions, give the money to the poor, and come and follow Him. The young man leaves disappointed. Jesus tells the disciples, "I tell you the truth, it is hard for a rich man to enter the kingdom of heaven" (Matt. 19:16–23). To reinforce His answer, Jesus utters an enigmatic saying that has puzzled believers for centuries: "Again I tell you, it is easier for a camel to go through the eye of a needle than for a rich man to enter the kingdom of God" (Matt. 19:24).

This is one of the most commonly misunderstood sayings in the ministry of Jesus. There have been all kinds of theories brought forth to try to explain this puzzling comparison. Like many of the other teachings of Jesus, this one has been severely misunderstood because of our lack of understanding of first-century Jewish culture and idioms.

One of the most common explanations of this text is that there used to be a very low gate in Jerusalem called the eye of the needle.[5] It is said that the camel could not pass through the gate unless it stooped down on all fours and had all its baggage removed first. This makes a great sermon illustration for sure—that in order to come to God, we must first fall to our knees and remove all of our baggage before coming into His presence. Great illustration, but unfortunately, it's unfounded.

It is important to state that no such gate has ever been found in any archaeological excavation. Also, you have to think through the theory of a small gate. It just doesn't make any sense. In ancient Israel the camel was one of the main ways to travel long distances. Because Jerusalem was home to the Temple, it was a very transient city, with travelers coming and going from all over the world to celebrate the Passover and the other biblical holidays. Why would anyone who knows full well that camels would be coming in and out of the city on a regular basis build such a small gate? To do so would be foolishness.

There are two key words that have to be examined in order to come to the proper interpretation and understanding of this passage. They are the words "camel" and "needle." We can understand the needle if we go back to the original language of the New Testament, Greek. The word used for needle is *rhaphis*.

The Greek text also sheds some light on the word for "camel." It is possible that the wrong word was used in translation because of the similarity of the spelling in the Greek language. The word *kamelos* means "camel," while the word *kamilos* means "cable or rope." This helps to clarify what Jesus was actually saying. We can, however, go a step further.

We know that Jesus probably spoke in Aramaic, an ancient Semitic language used in the Middle East for centuries. The Ancient Aramaic word is *gamla* and is the same word for both "camel" and "rope."[6]

So with this new information we can see we do not have to explain away the meaning of this teaching. In fact, it is very clear what Jesus was trying to teach. The text could read something like this then: "Again I tell you, it is easier for a rope to go through the eye of a needle than for a rich man to enter the kingdom of God." So Jesus is saying it is virtually impossible for a rich man to enter God's kingdom. Thankfully, just two verses later Jesus says, "With man this is impossible, but with God all things are possible" (Matt. 19:26).

The Fourth Messianic Miracle—the Raising of Lazarus after Four Days

While on His way to Jerusalem with the disciples, Jesus learns that His friend Lazarus is sick. They make their way to Bethany to the east of the city in order to minister to him, although Jesus knows already that Lazarus has died.

This brings us to the fourth and final Messianic miracle of Jesus. It is so powerful when you understand the Hebraic significance of this passage. Let's take a look at the Scripture in John 11:1–44:

> Now a man named Lazarus was sick. He was from Bethany, the village of Mary and her sister Martha. This Mary, whose brother Lazarus now lay sick, was the same one who poured perfume on the Lord and wiped his feet with her hair. So the sisters sent word to Jesus, "Lord, the one you love is sick." When he heard this, Jesus said, "This sickness will not end in death. No, it is for God's glory so that God's Son may be glorified through it."
>
> Jesus loved Martha and her sister and Lazarus. Yet when he heard that Lazarus was sick, he stayed where he was two more days. Then he said to his disciples, "Let us go back to Judea." "But Rabbi," they said, "a short while ago the Jews tried to stone you, and yet you are going back there?" Jesus answered, "Are there not twelve hours of daylight? A man who walks by day will not stumble, for he sees by this world's light.

It is when he walks by night that he stumbles, for he has no light."

After he had said this, he went on to tell them, "Our friend Lazarus has fallen asleep; but I am going there to wake him up." His disciples replied, "Lord, if he sleeps, he will get better." Jesus had been speaking of his death, but his disciples thought he meant natural sleep. So then he told them plainly, "Lazarus is dead, and for your sake I am glad I was not there, so that you may believe. But let us go to him." Then Thomas (called Didymus) said to the rest of the disciples, "Let us also go, that we may die with him."

On his arrival, Jesus found that Lazarus had already been in the tomb for four days. Bethany was less than two miles from Jerusalem, and many Jews had come to Martha and Mary to comfort them in the loss of their brother. When Martha heard that Jesus was coming, she went out to meet him, but Mary stayed at home.

"Lord," Martha said to Jesus, "if you had been here, my brother would not have died. But I know that even now God will give you whatever you ask." Jesus said to her, "Your brother will rise again." Martha answered, "I know he will rise again in the resurrection at the last day." Jesus said to her, "I am the resurrection and the life. He who believes in me will live, even though he dies; and whoever lives and believes in me will never die. Do you believe this?" "Yes, Lord," she told him, "I believe that you are the Christ, the Son of God, who was to come into the world." And after she had said this, she went back and called her sister Mary aside. "The Teacher is here," she said, "and is asking for you." When Mary heard this, she got up quickly and went to him.

Now Jesus had not yet entered the village, but was still at the place where Martha had met him. When the Jews who had been with Mary in the house, comforting her, noticed how quickly she got up and went out, they followed her, supposing she was going to the tomb to mourn there. When Mary reached the place where Jesus was and saw him, she fell at his feet and said, "Lord, if you had been here, my brother would not have died." When Jesus saw her weeping, and the Jews who had come along with her also weeping, he was deeply moved in spirit and troubled. "Where have you laid him?" he asked. "Come and see, Lord," they replied. Jesus wept. Then the Jews said, "See how he loved him!" But some of them said, "Could not he who opened the eyes of the blind man have kept this man from dying?"

Jesus, once more deeply moved, came to the tomb. It was a cave with a stone laid across the entrance. "Take away the stone," he said. "But, Lord," said Martha, the sister of the dead man, "by this time there is a bad odor, for he has been there four days." Then Jesus said, "Did I not tell you that if you believed, you would see the glory of God?" So they took away the stone. Then Jesus looked up and said, "Father, I thank you that you have heard me. I knew that you always hear me, but I said this for the benefit of the people standing here, that they may believe that you sent me." When he had said this, Jesus called in a loud

> voice, "Lazarus, come out!" The dead man came out, his hands and feet wrapped with strips of linen, and a cloth around his face. Jesus said to them, "Take off the grave clothes and let him go."

What an incredible story! For many it is a great source of strength to believe in God for the impossible. There is also a Hebraic influence in this passage that brings it to life. The rabbis taught that resurrection from the dead was only possible within the first three days.[7] The belief was that the spirit of a person would hover over the body for the first three days after death. During that time, if one was empowered by God to do so, resurrection was possible. But only the Messiah could perform a resurrection on or after the fourth day. With that idea in mind, let's reexamine the story of Lazarus.

Strange as it may seem, it is almost as if Jesus went out of His way to be late once he learned that Lazarus was sick. We read: "Jesus loved Martha and her sister and Lazarus. Yet when he heard that Lazarus was sick, he stayed where he was two more days. Then he said to his disciples, 'Let us go back to Judea'" (John 11:5–6). It wasn't that Jesus did not care about Lazarus. In fact, the text says that Jesus loved Martha and her sister and Lazarus. Rather, Jesus knew that God had a purpose to accomplish through Lazarus. Jesus said, "This sickness will not end in death. No, it is for God's glory so that God's Son may be glorified through it" (John 11:4).

Jesus and His disciples go to Bethany, where He meets the sisters who are grieving because Lazarus has died. By the time Jesus arrives, Lazarus has been buried for four days. Jesus then goes to the grave of His friend and is obviously deeply moved by Lazarus's death and the grief of his family. The reaction of the people at the grave is interesting to note. When Jesus arrived, there was not one person who thought He would do what He did—they all thought He was just being a good friend. Notice what they said: "Could not he who opened the eyes of the blind man have kept this man from dying?" That statement suggests to us the people's attitude toward Jesus. Their statement implies that He was the Messiah. "Didn't He do other Messianic miracles already?" was what they were saying. Of course Jesus was fully aware of the beliefs of his fellow Jews concerning the Messiah. When He asked them to remove the stone, He was declaring His Messiahship in a clear, loud voice and everyone who was there that day knew it.

Imagine the tension and excitement of that moment. Many had made the claim to be the One, but here was this man, Jesus of Nazareth, supporting His claims with miracle after miracle. When Lazarus came out of the tomb alive and well on the fourth day, there was no denying the truth from that moment on—Jesus was the promised Messiah. That is what John tells us: "Therefore many of the Jews who had come to visit Mary, and had seen what Jesus did, put their faith in him" (John 11:45).

This fourth and final Messianic miracle was the proverbial nail in the coffin for Jesus. Consider the text that followed Lazarus's resurrection from the dead in

John 11:53: "So from that day on they plotted to take his [Jesus'] life." The rabbis, the Pharisees, and Israel itself could not deny it or question it any longer. They had to either accept Him as Messiah or do away with Him as quickly as they could. History records their choice.

Chapter 5

The Final Week in Jerusalem

Jesus is now approaching the most important week of His life, the Passion Week. We know this is so important because the Gospel writers devote a disproportionate amount of space to it. Mark's Gospel, for example, spends five out of sixteen chapters describing the events of this single week out of the three years Jesus probably spent in ministry.

We know from the words of Jesus that He understood the appointment with divine destiny that awaited Him in the Holy City. Mark writes:

> They were on their way up to Jerusalem, with Jesus leading the way, and the disciples were astonished, while those who followed were afraid. Again he took the Twelve aside and told them what was going to happen to him. "We are going up to Jerusalem," he said, "and the Son of Man will be betrayed to the chief priests and teachers of the law. They will condemn him to death and will hand him over to the Gentiles, who

> will mock him and spit on him, flog him and kill him. Three days later he will rise." (Mark 10:32–34)

Jesus Himself told His disciples, "In any case, I must keep going today and tomorrow and the next day—for surely no prophet can die outside Jerusalem!" (Luke 13:33). This momentous week begins with His formal arrival in the city, an event we now commemorate on Palm Sunday.

The Triumphal Entry

Many will remember the colorful story of Jesus' ride into Jerusalem on a donkey. Matthew describes it for us:

> As they approached Jerusalem and came to Bethphage on the Mount of Olives, Jesus sent two disciples, saying to them, "Go to the village ahead of you, and at once you will find a donkey tied there, with her colt by her. Untie them and bring them to me. If anyone says anything to you, tell him that the Lord needs them, and he will send them right away." This took place to fulfill what was spoken through the prophet: "Say to the Daughter of Zion, 'See, your king comes to you, gentle and riding on a donkey, on a colt, the foal of a donkey.'" The disciples went and did as Jesus had instructed them. They brought the donkey and the colt, placed their cloaks on them, and Jesus sat on them.

> A very large crowd spread their cloaks on the road, while others cut branches from the trees and spread them on the road. The crowds that went ahead of him and those that followed shouted, "Hosanna to the Son of David! Blessed is he who comes in the name of the Lord! Hosanna in the highest!" When Jesus entered Jerusalem, the whole city was stirred and asked, "Who is this?" Crowds answered, "This is Jesus, the prophet from Nazareth in Galilee." (Matt. 21:1–11)

Have you ever read this familiar story of the "Triumphant Entry" of Jesus into Jerusalem and wondered, *How was it that on that exact day and during that exact moment when Jesus rode into Jerusalem through the Eastern Gate there was a huge crowd standing there with branches in their hands just waiting to welcome the Messiah?* Without proper understanding of ancient Jewish culture and Temple practices we miss the beauty and power of this momentous day in the ministry of Jesus.

As we will see in the later section "The Feast of Passover," all the lambs for the Passover came from Bethlehem.[1] The High Priest would go down from Jerusalem to Bethlehem and find a perfect lamb. After selecting the lamb he would carry it back to the city and through the Eastern Gate on the tenth day of the Hebrew month of Nissan—four days before the Passover. As he would carry the lamb through the Temple area, the people would gather with palm branches and sing praises to the Lord. They would shout, "Hosanna to the lamb of God who has come to take our sins away!" This explains why the crowd was at the Eastern Gate, their palm branches in hand, when Jesus entered. In fact, Matthew tells us that the crowd actually met Jesus on the road as He was approaching the city. John adds that the crowd went out to meet Jesus because they had heard that Jesus had performed the Messianic sign of raising Lazarus after four days in the grave (John 12:18).

This background information helps us to understand the significance of what happened to Jesus that day. In essence you have Jesus, the Lamb of God, Who was declared to be the Messiah by John the Baptist—who belonged to the family of the High Priest—being carried on a donkey through the Eastern Gate probably just behind the High Priest as he entered with the Passover lamb. Jesus of Nazareth, Who has performed all of the required Messianic miracles and has fulfilled all other required prophecies to be the Messiah, is greeted by a crowd who are rejoicing because the sacrificial lamb of God for the Passover Feast has been selected.

It is also significant that Jesus comes riding in on a donkey. Let's look at the passage Matthew quotes as he tells this story, Zechariah 9:9: "Shout, Daughter of Jerusalem! See, your king comes to you, righteous and having salvation, gentle and riding on a donkey, on a colt, the foal of a donkey."

This passage calls upon Israel to rejoice because her king will come to her bringing salvation and riding on a donkey. The people cry out, "Hosanna to the Son of David!" This phrase "Son of David" was the most common title used for the Messiah in Jesus' day. The word "Hosanna," which is taken from a key Messianic Psalm, literally means "Save now!" (Ps. 118:25). It later became a word of blessing or acclamation, as it is used here.

Even the choice of mount on which Jesus rode is significant. In ancient times, when a king came into a neighboring country on a mission of peace he would come riding a donkey.[2] However, if he came to make war against that nation, then he would come riding a horse. We can see this in Revelation 19:11: "I saw heaven standing open and there before me was a white horse, whose rider is called Faithful and True. With justice he judges and makes war." It's awesome to realize that the first time Jesus came to earth He came riding a donkey on a mission of peace, yet when He returns to earth the second time He will be riding a horse to make war against the nations.

The fact that Jesus came through the Eastern Gate is important. There are several gates into the city. Why did Jesus ride in through that one in particular? There were probably two reasons. First, the Eastern Gate is on the road from Bethany into Jerusalem and we know that Jesus was staying in Bethany. Second, consider the words of the prophet in Ezekiel 44:1–2: "Then the man brought me back to the outer gate of the sanctuary, the one facing east, and it was shut. The Lord said to me, 'This gate is to remain shut. It must not be opened; no one may enter through it. It is to remain shut because the Lord, the God of Israel, has entered through it.'" Ezekiel said one day God would enter

Jerusalem through the Eastern Gate of the city and after that day they were to shut or seal the gate so that no one would be able to enter through it again.

If you have ever been to Jerusalem or have seen a picture of the Eastern Gate today you know it is completely sealed up and no one may enter through it. In fact, there is a Muslim graveyard in front of it blocking the entrance. So if the gate is sealed up just as the Bible says, then God Himself must have entered through that gate. When did that happen? It happened the day Jesus entered Jerusalem riding upon the back of a donkey. The gate has been sealed up for all time until the day the Messiah will return and walk through it once again.

After the sacrificial lamb was selected by the High Priest and carried through the Eastern Gate it was tied to the entrance of the Temple for all to inspect it.[3] They had to make sure that it was without blemish, that it was perfect and faultless. This would continue for four days until the twilight hours leading up to Passover.

Jesus comes into Jerusalem on the tenth day of Nissan, four days before the Passover. He is then brought into the Temple and He is examined or inspected by all for a period of four days. He is examined by the Pharisees and the Sanhedrin. He is seen by Pontius Pilate and then Jesus is sent to Herod, who finds no fault with Him, so He is sent back to Pilate. After four days and after Jesus being "tied to the entrance of the Temple," so to speak, Pilate declares, "I can find no fault with this man." Jesus, the perfect Lamb of God, is declared worthy to be the Passover Lamb.

Taxes to Caesar

While Jesus was teaching in the Temple during Passover week, the authorities tried to trick Him into saying something that would allow them to have Him arrested. This is the context of this familiar saying found in Luke 20:20–26:

> So they watched [for an opportunity to ensnare] Him, and sent spies who pretended to be upright (honest and sincere), that they might lay hold of something He might say, so as to turn Him over to the control and authority of the governor. They asked Him, "Teacher, we know that You speak and teach what is right, and that You show no partiality to anyone but teach the way of God honestly and in truth. Is it lawful for us to give tribute to Caesar or not?"
>
> But He recognized and understood their cunning and unscrupulousness and said to them, "Show Me a denarius (a coin)! Whose image and inscription does it have?" They answered, "Caesar's." He said to them, "Then render to Caesar the things that are Caesar's, and to God the things that are God's." So they could not in the presence of the people take hold of anything He said to turn it against Him; but marveling at His reply, they were silent. (AMP)

This is one of those passages you read in the Scripture that give you the feeling you need to know more about what was going on in the background. Without any background information the passage can lose its intended message. These spies are sent by the religious leadership who want to trap Jesus so they can charge him before the local governor. The question has to do with paying taxes to the Roman authorities. If Jesus agreed to pay taxes to Caesar, then the spies would accuse him of being a traitor to Israel because of His support of thc Roman occupation. If He said not to pay, then the spies would go to the local authorities and accuse Jesus of teaching the people to disobey Roman law and therefore have Him charged. This seems to be a "lose-lose" situation for Jesus. However, Jesus gives one response that not only gets Him off the hook but silences His accusers as well. What exactly did He say or do to put them in their place?

To answer this question we need some understanding of first-century rabbinic law. First, we must look at the type of coin Jesus asked them for. He was very specific in the kind of coin He asked for. He asked them to show Him a denarius (which was a coin issued by the Romans). The verse implies that Jesus' accusers had one of these coins in their pouch. By the very fact that Jesus asked for that specific coin He was showing the people around Him these men were in possession of such a coin. This particular coin bore the image of Caesar the deified emperor who reigned over most of the known world.

These spies came to accuse Jesus and trap Him into breaking the law. The fact of the matter is that it was these very accusers of Jesus who were breaking the law. The fact they were carrying this particular coin was in direct violation of the Torah. This is what the Bible says about images in Deuteronomy 4:15–16: "You saw no form of any kind the day the Lord spoke to you at Horeb out of the fire. Therefore watch yourselves very carefully, so that you do not become corrupt and make for yourselves an idol, an image of any shape, whether formed like a man or a woman."

This Scripture forbids God's people from making for themselves an image to worship. Since the Roman emperor was worshiped as a god, his image stamped on the denarius was viewed as an idol. The last thing a faithful Jew would do is bring an idol into the Temple of the Lord. The intensity of feeling over this issue was well illustrated by an incident in the early years of Pilate's rule in Judea (AD 26–36). A cohort of his troops entered Jerusalem with images of the emperor attached to their standards and put them in the Antonia Fortress right next to the Temple. This was considered a desecration of the Temple, since it involved bringing objects used in pagan worship onto the Temple hill. A huge multitude of ordinary Jews protested to the governor at his residence in Caesarea, saying they were willing to die if the standard was not removed. Pilate relented.[4]

In answering their question, Jesus did what the rabbis often did, He responded to their question with another question. Holding up the coin, He asked whose image was stamped on it. The answer, of course, was "Caesar's image." Jesus then gave an answer that bypassed the false assumption contained in the original question, that it was impossible to serve God faithfully and obey the emperor. He said to give the emperor what is his (taxes) and to give God what belongs to Him (worship, obedience, faithfulness, and so forth). This incident demonstrates how well-versed Jesus was in the rabbinic way of thinking. He was able to defend Himself against attack by demonstrating the hypocrisy of his opponents and that their assumptions regarding serving God were false. He "showed them up" at their own game, as it were.

The Feast of Passover

There is no other event in the life of Jesus that is so powerfully depicted in the Jewish feasts as His sacrifice for our sins on the cross. Paul literally calls Jesus "our Passover" (1 Cor. 5:7). Let's look into this biblical celebration that points unerringly to the Lamb of God Who takes away the sin of the world:

> The Lord said to Moses and Aaron in Egypt, "This month is to be for you the first month, the first month of your year. Tell the whole community of Israel that on the tenth day of this month each man is to take a lamb for his family, one for each household. If any household is too small for a whole lamb, they must share one with their nearest neighbor, having taken into account the number of people there are. You are to determine the amount of lamb needed in accordance with what each person will eat. The animals you

choose must be year-old males without defect, and you may take them from the sheep or the goats. Take care of them until the fourteenth day of the month, when all the people of the community of Israel must slaughter them at twilight.

"Then they are to take some of the blood and put it on the sides and tops of the doorframes of the houses where they eat the lambs. That same night they are to eat the meat roasted over the fire, along with bitter herbs, and bread made without yeast. Do not eat the meat raw or cooked in water, but roast it over the fire—head, legs and inner parts. Do not leave any of it till morning; if some is left till morning, you must burn it.

"This is how you are to eat it: with your cloak tucked into your belt, your sandals on your feet and your staff in your hand. Eat it in haste; it is the Lord's Passover. On that same night I will pass through Egypt and strike down every firstborn—both men and animals—and I will bring judgment on all the gods of Egypt. I am the Lord. The blood will be a sign for you on the houses where you are; and when I see the blood, I will pass over you. No destructive plague will touch you when I strike Egypt.

"This is a day you are to commemorate; for the generations to come you shall celebrate it as a festival to the Lord—a lasting ordinance. For seven days you are to eat bread made without yeast. On the first day remove the yeast from your houses, for whoever eats anything with yeast in it from the first day through the seventh must be cut off from Israel. On the first day hold a sacred assembly, and another one on the seventh day. Do no work at all on these days, except to prepare food for everyone to eat—that is all you may do.

"Celebrate the Feast of Unleavened Bread, because it was on this very day that I brought your divisions out of Egypt. Celebrate this day as a lasting ordinance for the generations to come. In the first month you are to eat bread made without yeast, from the evening of the fourteenth day until the evening of the twenty-first day. For seven days no yeast is to be found in your houses. And whoever eats anything with yeast in it must be cut off from the community of Israel, whether he is an alien or native-born. Eat nothing made with yeast. Wherever you live, you must eat unleavened bread."

Then Moses summoned all the elders of Israel and said to them, "Go at once and select the animals for your families and slaughter the Passover lamb. Take a bunch of hyssop, dip it into the blood in the basin and put some of the blood on the top and on both sides of the doorframe. Not one of you shall go out the door of his house until morning. When the Lord goes through the land to strike down the Egyptians, he will see the blood on the top and sides of the doorframe and will pass over that doorway, and he will not permit the destroyer to enter your houses and strike you down.

"Obey these instructions as a lasting ordinance for you and your descendants. When you enter the land that the Lord will give you as he promised, observe this ceremony. And when your children ask you,

'What does this ceremony mean to you?' then tell them, 'It is the Passover sacrifice to the Lord, who passed over the houses of the Israelites in Egypt and spared our homes when he struck down the Egyptians.'"

Then the people bowed down and worshiped. The Israelites did just what the Lord commanded Moses and Aaron. At midnight the Lord struck down all the firstborn in Egypt, from the firstborn of Pharaoh, who sat on the throne, to the firstborn of the prisoner, who was in the dungeon, and the firstborn of all the livestock as well.

Pharaoh and all his officials and all the Egyptians got up during the night, and there was loud wailing in Egypt, for there was not a house without someone dead. During the night Pharaoh summoned Moses and Aaron and said, "Up! Leave my people, you and the Israelites! Go, worship the Lord as you have requested. Take your flocks and herds, as you have said, and go. And also bless me."

The Egyptians urged the people to hurry and leave the country. "For otherwise," they said, "we will all die!" So the people took their dough before the yeast was added, and carried it on their shoulders in kneading troughs wrapped in clothing. The Israelites did as Moses instructed and asked the Egyptians for articles of silver and gold and for clothing. The Lord had made the Egyptians favorably disposed toward the people, and they gave them what they asked for; so they plundered the Egyptians.

The Israelites journeyed from Rameses to Succoth.

There were about six hundred thousand men on foot, besides women and children. Many other people went up with them, as well as large droves of livestock, both flocks and herds. With the dough they had brought from Egypt, they baked cakes of unleavened bread. The dough was without yeast because they had been driven out of Egypt and did not have time to prepare food for themselves.

Now the length of time the Israelite people lived in Egypt was 430 years. At the end of the 430 years, to the very day, all the Lord's divisions left Egypt. Because the Lord kept vigil that night to bring them out of Egypt, on this night all the Israelites are to keep vigil to honor the Lord for the generations to come.

The Lord said to Moses and Aaron, "These are the regulations for the Passover: No foreigner is to eat of it. Any slave you have bought may eat of it after you have circumcised him, but a temporary resident and a hired worker may not eat of it. It must be eaten inside one house; take none of the meat outside the house. Do not break any of the bones. The whole community of Israel must celebrate it.

"An alien living among you who wants to celebrate the Lord's Passover must have all the males in his household circumcised; then he may take part like one born in the land. No uncircumcised male may eat of it. The same law applies to the native-born and to the alien living among you." All the Israelites did just what the Lord had commanded Moses and Aaron. And on that very day the Lord brought the Israelites out of Egypt by their divisions. (Exod. 12:1–51)

This is where it all begins. Passover was the first feast to be established (the details of the others came later in time). Passover is foundational and cannot be overlooked when it comes to studying the prophetic nature of the feasts. There are many parallels between the life and death of the Passover lamb and Jesus, God's Passover Lamb.

The name for Passover in Hebrew is Pesach; it simply means to "pass over."[5] The name of this feast is rooted in the manner in which God said He would protect the Israelites from His final and most powerful plague—the killing of the firstborn male in every home. God said He would send an angel of death to every home in the land. All firstborn sons would be killed except for those whose families applied the blood of the lamb to the doorposts of their home in the manner in which He would prescribe.

At this stage it's important to note that we should always pay attention to the details of the Scriptures in both the Old and the New Testaments. We have to remember the authors were Jewish and were writing to a Jewish audience. Keeping that in mind, let's begin our journey by paralleling the requirements for the Passover lamb and the life of the Messiah, Jesus.

The first thing we will look at is what I call the letter of blood. In Exodus 12:7 God instructed the Israelites to apply the blood to the doorframes in a very specific manner. He said they were to apply it to the sides and the top of the doorframe. What not everyone knows is that by applying the blood in that manner we are left with the letter *chet* in the Hebrew alphabet. It is the eighth letter and carries the meaning "life." It's amazing to see that God would embed this symbol into the very first command He gives in regard to the Passover Feast. When the angel of death came to a house that had the letter of life on it, it had to "Passover" the house. Death cannot come to where God has placed life.

There is a question that we need to ask ourselves: Have we applied the blood to our doorposts? Have we applied the blood over our marriages, our children, and others whom we love and care for? Know that as long as you have His life applied, by faith, to the doorposts of your home the destroyer cannot and will not come in. Every time you face an attack or a difficult circumstance, just turn to the life-giving blood of the Lamb.

Though the command was given for the lamb to be killed publicly so that the entire assembly could witness it, the blood of the lamb had to be applied personally. There is so much power in that statement. We know that Jesus was the Lamb of God Who was slain once for all, so some would say then that we are all saved because He already died—that's universalism. The truth is, just like the lamb's blood had to be applied personally to every home, we, too, by faith, must apply the blood of the sacrifice of Jesus to the doorframes on our hearts.

The next parallel I want to look at is concerning the location the lambs for the Feast of Passover came from. All the lambs came from special fields in the town of Bethlehem, just five miles south of Jerusalem.[6] Contained within these fields were the pure and spotless lambs. Once we have this picture in our minds, it causes us to stop and wonder if on the night Jesus was born it was the shepherds who worked in these special fields to whom the angels appeared and made their Messianic proclamation about His birth.

Bethlehem consists of two Hebrew words, *beit* and *lechem*, which literally means "house of bread." On several occasions, Jesus told the people He was the Bread of Life that had come down from heaven (John 6:35). What more appropriate town for Jesus—the Bread of Life—to be born in than Bethlehem?

Consider also what the prophet Micah said concerning the birth of the Messiah in Micah 5:2: "But you, Bethlehem Ephrathah, though you are small among the clans of Judah, out of you will come for me one who will be ruler over Israel, whose origins are from of old, from ancient times." It was prophesied that the Messiah would come from this little insignificant shepherding village of Bethlehem, the same as the Passover lambs.

It was the duty and right of the High Priest of Israel to select and declare the Passover lamb for sacrifice.[7] He would go down to Bethlehem to select a pure and spotless lamb. We know Jesus was the Passover Lamb of God, but which High Priest selected Him and where was He presented to Israel as the pure and spotless Lamb? John the Baptist performed this role on the day of Jesus' immersion. Luke 1:5 says: "In the time of Herod king of Judea there was a priest named Zechariah, who belonged to the priestly division of Abijah; his wife Elizabeth was also a descendant of Aaron."

John's father and mother were both from the line of Aaron, so they are descendants of the Aaronic Priesthood (the High Priests of Israel). So John the Baptist is from the lineage of the High Priest of Israel and has the right and duty to select the Passover Lamb for sacrifice. Jesus comes to him at the Jordan River and John makes the declaration in John 1:29–31: "The next day John saw Jesus coming toward him and said, 'Look, the Lamb of God, who takes away the sin of the world! This is the one I meant when I said, "A man who comes after me has surpassed me because he was before me." I myself did not know him, but the reason I came baptizing with water was that he might be revealed to Israel.'" So as a descendant of the High Priest John had the right to declare the Lamb for sacrifice. He sees Jesus and he points it out for all to see who were assembled in that place.

John the Baptist was also born at Passover (see chapter 1). The time of his birth is of great prophetic significance for us. The Jewish people believed that the prophet Elijah would come before the appearance of the Messiah on earth. This comes from a Messianic prophecy in Malachi 4:5: "See, I will send you the prophet Elijah before that great and dreadful day of the Lord comes."

Even today during the Passover Seder or dinner, a special seat and glass is set apart for Elijah. The hope is that he will come on that day. During the dinner a child is sent to open up the front door in hopes that Elijah will come to the door and announce the coming of the Messiah and that he will tell them Who He is.

Therefore, John—as the Elijah figure who is born

at Passover—declares to Israel Who their Messiah is. John chooses Jesus of Nazareth. Jesus affirmed John's role as Elijah in Matthew 11:13-15: "For all the Prophets and the Law prophesied until John. And if you are willing to accept it, he is the Elijah who was to come. He who has ears let him hear." So we can see how God was sovereignly working in the background to have all things fulfilled so that there would be no denying His Son was indeed the spotless Passover Lamb Who would be slain for the sins of the world.

Jesus in the Garden

Following the Last Supper with His disciples, Jesus walks with them through Jerusalem and across the Kidron Valley to the Mount of Olives, where they take refuge in a garden so the Master can pray. Mark records the scene:

> He went a little farther, and fell on the ground, and prayed that if it were possible, the hour might pass from Him. And He said, "Abba, Father, all things are possible for You. Take this cup away from Me; nevertheless, not what I will, but what You will." (Mark 14:35–36 NKJV)

The "cup" Jesus refers to in His prayer goes back to the Last Supper He has just celebrated with His disciples as described by Luke:

> When the hour came, Jesus and his apostles reclined at the table. And he said to them, "I have eagerly desired to eat this Passover with you before I suffer. For I tell you, I will not eat it again until it finds fulfillment in the kingdom of God." After taking the cup, he gave thanks and said, "Take this and divide it among you. For I tell you I will not drink again of the fruit of the vine until the kingdom of God comes." And he took bread, gave thanks and broke it, and gave it to them, saying, "This is my body given for you; do this in remembrance of me." In the same way, after the supper he took the cup, saying, "This cup is the new covenant in my blood, which is poured out for you." (Luke 22:14–20)

This is the point of no return. If Jesus was going to back out of His mission, this was the time to do it. If He chose to continue from this moment forward, then there would be no way out. After a lifetime of preparation, it all came down to this one moment, this one prayer: "Take this cup away from Me." Most commentators refer to this cup that Jesus is asking to be removed as a cup of bitterness, because of the pain that He was about to endure. While this is totally possible, there is also another explanation, a much more significant explanation in my view. The explanation for His choice of words here is once again found in the Feasts of the Lord.

Where was Jesus just before the garden? He was in the upper room with His disciples, where they had just finished eating the Passover meal. We need to be aware of the richness of imagery that is found in this Passover meal, which in Hebrew is called a seder. The Passover meal, as found in Luke, speaks of various cups. At first glance this seems to be of no significance. But this is not the case. Why are the cups so important?

They are important because the Passover meal that Jesus ate with His disciples that night was not so different from the Passover that is celebrated today. Granted, today there are different foods than what they used, but the basic outline of the service known as the seder is the same. During the meal there are four cups that are drunk throughout the evening. They are: the Cup of Sanctification, the Cup of Thanks, the Cup of Redemption, and the Cup of Acceptance.

Notice that the third cup is called the Cup of Redemption. You drink this cup after supper, which is precisely when the text in Luke says that Jesus took the cup and declared that from that moment on it would be the cup of the New Covenant. Jesus took the third cup of the seder, the Cup of Redemption, and declared that this cup filled with wine would now represent the redeeming blood that He was about to shed. When He prayed in the garden and asked the Father if the cup could pass from Him, He was referring to this cup that pointed toward His death for our sins. If He did not accept the Cup of Redemption by pouring out His blood, there could be no salvation for anyone.

Pilate Washes His Hands of Jesus

After His arrest, Jesus is taken to the Jewish Council, the Sanhedrin, and then sent on to Pilate as a rebel against Rome. Pilate interviews Him, learns He is from Galilee, then sends Him to Herod Antipas, who ruled Galilee and Perea and was probably in Jerusalem for the Passover Feast. Herod tries to interview Jesus, Who refuses to respond, so he has Jesus returned to Pilate. After hearing the accusations of the Jewish leaders against Jesus, Pilate decides He is innocent and tries to release Him. The Jews call for His death, and when the situation begins to get out of hand Pilate gives in to them and turns Jesus over to be crucified. This brings us to the curious incident at the conclusion of the trial where Pilate washes his hands:

> Now it was the governor's custom at the Feast to release a prisoner chosen by the crowd. At that time they had a notorious prisoner, called Barabbas. So when the crowd had gathered, Pilate asked them, "Which one do you want me to release to you: Barabbas, or Jesus who is called Christ?" For he knew it was out of envy that they had handed Jesus over to him. While Pilate was sitting on the judge's seat, his wife sent him this message: "Don't have anything to do with that innocent man, for I have suffered a great deal today in a dream because of him." But the chief priests and the elders persuaded the crowd to ask for Barabbas and to have Jesus executed. "Which of the two

> do you want me to release to you?" asked the governor. "Barabbas," they answered. "What shall I do, then, with Jesus who is called Christ?" Pilate asked. They all answered, "Crucify him!" "Why? What crime has he committed?" asked Pilate. But they shouted all the louder, "Crucify him!" When Pilate saw that he was getting nowhere, but that instead an uproar was starting, he took water and washed his hands in front of the crowd. "I am innocent of this man's blood," he said. "It is your responsibility!" All the people answered, "Let his blood be on us and on our children!" Then he released Barabbas to them. But he had Jesus flogged, and handed him over to be crucified. Then the governor's soldiers took Jesus into the Praetorium and gathered the whole company of soldiers around him. They stripped him and put a scarlet robe on him, and then twisted together a crown of thorns and set it on his head. They put a staff in his right hand and knelt in front of him and mocked him. "Hail, king of the Jews!" they said. They spit on him, and took the staff and struck him on the head again and again. After they had mocked him, they took off the robe and put his own clothes on him. Then they led him away to crucify him. (Matt. 27:15–31)

While the trial of Jesus is present in all the Gospel accounts, it's no surprise that Matthew is the one who includes the part about Pilate washing his hands (Deut. 21:6–7). As we will see, Pilate's actions are very much consistent with first-century Passover practices. We know that Matthew is Jewish and that his primary audience is a Jewish one. His inclusion of Pilate's washing of the hands was a very direct message to the Jewish people of that day. Throughout the life of Jesus we have already seen many parallels between history and the requirements for the Passover Lamb. Even here, one tradition points to the fact that He was not only the Messiah but also the chosen Lamb of God.

There were many requirements given by God in preparing to sacrifice the Passover lamb for your family. After an intense inspection of the lamb and once you were satisfied that it had no fault or blemish, the one who was in charge of the lamb would wash his hands and then hand over the animal to be sacrificed. Matthew obviously had this tradition in mind when writing his account of Jesus' trial before Pilate. What a beautiful picture. After an intense process, Pilate—who was over the Lamb as the governor and His trial judge—declared Jesus to be without fault. Pilate then washed his hands and handed Jesus over to be sacrificed. The parallel is striking.[8]

There is one more important thing to note about Jesus' trial before Pilate. It is in regard to the crowd that was there in the court. Both Hollywood and tradition would have us believe that almost all of Jerusalem was present on that occasion demanding that Jesus be crucified. This is simply not the case. One has to remember that this is Pilate we are talking about. He was the Roman procurator of Judea. In today's terminology he would be equal to a provincial premier or state governor. This event took place in the Praetorium, also known as the Antonia Fortress. Its very name implies that it was a heavily guarded and fortified area. There is no way that it would have been open to the public. Given how unpopular Pilate was, due in large part to his total insensitivity to the religious convictions of his Jewish subjects, allowing a large crowd into his presence might have put his life at risk. It is highly unlikely that it happened that way. Most likely only the members of the Sanhedrin and a few carefully selected prominent men were present. It was a very small segment of the Jewish religious establishment who called for Jesus' crucifixion. The idea that all of Israel and all Jewish people are responsible for His death is completely false both historically and politically.

It is also untrue spiritually. Every true follower of Christ knows exactly what sent Jesus to the cross. Our sin! That and nothing else made it *inevitable* that He had to die if we were to be reconciled to God. Certainly the Jewish leaders were jealous and felt threatened by Jesus and so they plotted and accused. Governor Pilate also bears a good portion of the blame for spinelessly condemning a man he himself said was innocent. In the last analysis, however, the Bible states unequivocally that it was God's purpose for Jesus to die for the sins of the world. On the Day of Pentecost Peter says Jesus was "delivered up according to the definite and fixed purpose and settled plan and foreknowledge of God" (Acts 2:23 NASB). Jesus went to the cross willingly out of His unfathomable love for us, and for His Father to fulfill His incredible rescue plan on behalf of His lost sons and daughters.

Chapter 6

Crucifixion to Pentecost

The Feast of Passover—the Crucifixion of God's Passover Lamb

In the previous chapter we looked at the details of the Passover celebration and compared them to the preparation of God's Lamb, Messiah Jesus. Now we look at the significance of the timing of Christ's death in relation to the Passover.

Following His mockery of a trial, Jesus is taken to the "Place of the Skull" outside Jerusalem and nailed to a crossbar, which is then hoisted up and fastened to a standing pole or sometimes a tree (Deut. 21:23; Gal. 3:13). This takes place at the "third hour" of the Jewish day, or at 9:00 in the morning for us. He hangs on the cross for six hours and then gives up His spirit and dies.

Matthew describes the scene:

> From noon to three, the whole earth was dark. Around mid-afternoon Jesus groaned out of the depths, crying loudly, "Eli, Eli, lama sabachthani?" which means, "My God, my God, why have you abandoned me?" Some bystanders who heard him said, "He's calling for Elijah." One of them ran and got a sponge soaked in sour wine and lifted it on a stick so he could drink. The others joked, "Don't be in such a hurry. Let's see if Elijah comes and saves him." But Jesus, again crying out loudly, breathed his last. (Matt. 27:45–50 The Message)

Why is the text so detailed in recounting the exact time of Jesus' death? The answer lies within our understanding of another powerful Passover tradition. Matthew, the Jewish disciple, in writing to a Jewish audience is compelled to relay this beautiful parallel. In the days of the Temple, the evening sacrifices took place at 3:00 p.m. Passover was no exception. At 3:00 p.m. on the day of Passover, the Lamb That the priest had chosen from Bethlehem—the Lamb for the nation—was sacrificed and presented to the people.[1]

The formal end to the Passover occurred when one of the priests would ascend the steps that led to the top of the walls of the Temple Mount. He would stand at the top of the southeast corner and at 3:00 p.m. he would blow the shofar in a specific series of blasts.[2] Why was the shofar used to announce the end of the feast? The answer is found back on Mount Sinai when God called Moses up to the mountain to give him the Ten Commandments. The story is told in Exodus 19:16–19:

> On the morning of the third day there was thunder and lightning, with a thick cloud over the mountain, and a very loud trumpet blast. Everyone in the camp trembled. Then Moses led the people out of the camp to meet with God, and they stood at the foot of the mountain. Mount Sinai was covered with smoke, because the Lord descended on it in fire. The smoke billowed up from it like smoke from a furnace, the whole mountain trembled violently, and the sound of the trumpet grew louder and louder. Then Moses spoke and the voice of God answered him.

Most English versions use the word "trumpet" in the account of the giving of the commandments. The trumpet used in this text is not the typical trumpet that we would think of in modern terms. The Hebrew word for trumpet is "shofar," which is a ram's horn. In this passage in Exodus, then, we see that the voice of God came in the form of a shofar blast to the people. Out of this passage arose a belief that the shofar was synonymous with the voice of God. Keeping this in mind, let's go back to the priest at Passover and his sounding of the shofar at 3:00 p.m. to bring Passover to a close. To those who heard the sound, it represented the voice of God declaring that His Passover Lamb had been sacrificed.

Not far from the Temple Mount, the crucified Jesus would also have heard the shofar blast. What did this blast mean to Him? Think about it. The sound of the shofar meant that the sacrifice had been completed; life had been secured. It is very possible that Jesus interpreted this trumpet blast as the voice of His Father declaring that Jesus' work of giving His life so that we might have life was finished. God had made His selection of His Lamb. The Lamb was sacrificed and now God was presenting Him for all to see.

This seems to explain why the Gospel records that it was precisely at 3:00 p.m. that Jesus cried out, "It is finished," and passed into His Father's presence.[3] Jesus had met all the requirements for the Passover Lamb once and for all. No more lambs needed to be sacrificed from that moment on. The Apostle Paul attests to this when he writes in I Corinthians 5:7b: "For Christ, our Passover lamb, has been sacrificed."

The Passover Lamb was to be of the firstborn; Jesus was the firstborn Son of God. We know that the Lamb's bones were not to be broken; none of Jesus' bones were broken. The parallels are overwhelming. We can have absolute confidence in the fact that Jesus of Nazareth truly was our Passover Lamb.

Even the location where the crucifixion took place has prophetic significance. Let's look backward in time to when the Lord spoke to Abraham in Genesis 22:2: "Then God said, 'Take your son, your only son, Isaac, whom you love, and go to the region of Moriah. Sacrifice him there as a burnt offering on one of the mountains I will tell you about.'" Abraham was told to sacrifice his son at Mount Moriah. We are told that because of Abraham's faith the Lord said He would provide a sacrifice one day. Then suddenly a ram appears in the thicket and Abraham sacrifices it in place of his son. This promise had dual significance. The first lamb was given right away to fulfill the first part of the promise. The rabbis always saw this promise of a lamb to also be prophetic in nature—that the lamb was a picture of the Messiah Who would come to be a sacrifice for them.

I have had the privilege of standing at the place of Jesus' crucifixion in Jerusalem. Some call it Calvary and yet some call it Golgotha—the Place of the Skull. What many people are not aware of is that Calvary is actually part of Mount Moriah. So even the place where Jesus died is the fulfillment of prophecy. Thousands of years before the death of Jesus, God promised Israel through Abraham that one day He would send them a Lamb for the sacrifice. It is on the very mount where God said He would provide the Lamb that Jesus, the Passover Lamb, is sacrificed. The truth can no longer be denied. Jesus is the Lamb of God and He truly is the Messiah.

The Bible records an incredible event that took place simultaneously in the Temple and on the cross. When Jesus died on the cross something amazing happened in the Temple. Let's read from Matthew 27:50–51: "And when Jesus had cried out again in a loud voice, he gave up his spirit. At that moment the curtain of the temple was torn in two from top to bottom. The earth shook and the rocks split." Why is this important and how does it affect us today? In both biblical and modern times, if a Jewish father lost his firstborn son he would tear his robe as a sign of grief and mourning.[4] Imagine what was happening in the minds and hearts of those who were celebrating the Passover at the Temple.

First of all, we must remember that Passover was a pilgrim feast, meaning that every Jewish male and his family were required to come to Jerusalem. So we know that the Temple would have been overflowing with people and activity. Only the priests would be inside the actual Temple building, in the Holy Place, which was separated from the Holy of Holies by a thick curtain or veil. Imagine that as they are worshiping God in the Temple, the Temple veil is torn in two before their very eyes, revealing the Holy of Holies where God's presence dwelt. The Glory of God is now exposed. They can see into the place where only the High Priest could go. God has just torn His robe because His Son has died! And in doing this, God has indicated that the way into His presence is now open for all because of the death of His Son (Heb. 10:19–22).

Who is this Son and where is He? They look to the cross and the one who is hanging upon it. They see Jesus Who claimed to be the Son of God. They see Jesus Who performed miracle after miracle. They see Jesus Who has fulfilled prophecy after prophecy in all that He has done. They see Jesus, the Son of God Who hangs upon the cross, Who has become their Passover Lamb. And as a sign to all of those present God tears His robe because He has just lost His Son! Wow!

It's noteworthy to mention that Passover is the only feast that God allowed the people to celebrate one month later. All other feasts had to be celebrated on the day that they were given. But Passover allows those who are unable to keep it at the prescribed time to celebrate it at a later date for whatever reason. Why would that be? Passover speaks of salvation. Without the shedding of the blood of the Lamb there is no salvation possible. What God, in His mercy, is saying to us is that it is never too late for us to come to salvation. All of our unsaved loved ones still have the opportunity to apply the blood to the doorposts of their hearts. Let us not grow weary in praying for those whom we long to see come to salvation. There is still power in the blood. And it is available to all who are searching.

The command from God in the Book of Exodus was to kill the lamb publicly so that all could witness its death. But each family had to apply the blood personally to their homes in order for salvation to come to them. If all the families did was go to the sacrificing ceremony and observe it and then go home without doing anything for themselves, surely death would have come to their home that night. They had to observe and then personally apply what had been done for them.

The same holds true for us today. Some people believe in universalism, that all will be saved in the end because Jesus died once for all, but that kind of thinking is foolishness and eternally dangerous. Yes, Jesus died once for all, but just as the Israelites had to apply the blood of the lamb to their homes, so we, too, must apply the sacrifice of Jesus' blood to the doorposts of our heart. If, by faith, we will apply His blood to our heart, then we, too, shall be saved from God's judgment for sin.

As we come to a close of our study on the Passover

there is one more area that is of value for us to examine. It concerns the progression of the power of the blood. When Abraham offered up the ram for Isaac, its blood was powerful enough to cover one young man. When the blood of the lamb was shed on the night of the Passover, its blood was powerful enough to cover an entire family. When the blood of the goats and lambs was shed on the great Day of Atonement, the blood was powerful enough to cover the sins of an entire nation. But then there came One Whose blood was more powerful than any that came before. It was the blood of Jesus of Nazareth of whom John the Baptist declared, "Behold the Lamb of God Who takes away the sin of the world!" The blood of Jesus is sufficient for the entire world. Not only that, His blood no longer *covers up* our sin like the blood of all those slain lambs before Him. His blood *takes away* our sin; He carries it away and removes it from us as far as the east is from the west (Ps. 103:12).

The Burial—the Feast of Unleavened Bread

Following the crucifixion, Jesus is removed from the cross and then laid in a borrowed tomb so as to avoid leaving the body exposed on the Sabbath, which signaled the start of the seven-day Feast of Unleavened Bread. To this feast we now turn.

The commandment to keep this feast is recorded in Exodus 12:14–20:

> This is a day you are to commemorate; for the generations to come you shall celebrate it as a festival to the Lord—a lasting ordinance. For seven days you are to eat bread made without yeast. On the first day remove the yeast from your houses, for whoever eats anything with yeast in it from the first day through the seventh must be cut off from Israel. On the first day hold a sacred assembly, and another one on the seventh day. Do no work at all on these days, except to prepare food for everyone to eat—that is all you may do. Celebrate the Feast of Unleavened Bread, because it was on this very day that I brought your divisions out of Egypt. Celebrate this day as a lasting ordinance for the generations to come. In the first month you are to eat bread made without yeast, from the evening of the fourteenth day until the evening of the twenty-first day. For seven days no yeast is to be found in your houses. And whoever eats anything with yeast in it must be cut off from the community of Israel, whether he is an alien or native-born. Eat nothing made with yeast. Wherever you live, you must eat unleavened bread.

This feast takes place on the fifteenth day of the Hebrew month of Nissan—exactly one day after the Passover—and it lasts for seven days. There are two major Messianic implications regarding this particular feast. The unleavened bread is a symbol of sinlessness, and the absence of decay in the bread points to resurrection. Let's start by taking a brief look at the origin of the feast.

This feast is an annual reminder of how quickly

God rescued His people out of Egyptian bondage. Although leaven is a picture of sin and is very much a part of this feast, I would like for us to consider another characteristic about the leaven and the escape from Egypt. Let's take a look at the passage in context before we examine this topic any further:

> During the night Pharaoh summoned Moses and Aaron and said, "Up! Leave my people, you and the Israelites! Go, worship the Lord as you have requested. Take your flocks and herds, as you have said, and go. And also bless me." The Egyptians urged the people to hurry and leave the country. "For otherwise," they said, "we will all die!" So the people took their dough before the yeast was added, and carried it on their shoulders in kneading troughs wrapped in clothing. The Israelites did as Moses instructed and asked the Egyptians for articles of silver and gold and for clothing. The Lord had made the Egyptians favorably disposed toward the people, and they gave them what they asked for; so they plundered the Egyptians. (Exod. 12:31–36)

Verse 34 is of great significance and is often overlooked by many people. The Bible records that God delivered His people out of slavery so quickly that they didn't even have time to add the leaven to their daily bread. What a powerful image. The Israelites were in bondage for 430 years. Every day it was the same thing, but on this day something happened that was different, something that was unexpected.

Perhaps you can identify with Israel at this point in their journey. Perhaps you have been praying for something for so long that just like the Israelites, you may have stopped believing it was going to happen. Every day they cried out to God for a deliverer to set them free from their oppressors and God, seemingly, did not reply. When they least expected it, when they were at their end and thought it would never happen, God came through for them. I want you to take courage; I want you to be strengthened. Never give up! Never stop believing! You serve a great and mighty God. You serve the God of Abraham, of Isaac, and of Jacob. Keep believing and pressing in. Know that your deliverance is sure and that it is near. As you pray and as you seek, He will deliver you. May your deliverance be as quick as it was for the Israelites.

God rescued the people so quickly they didn't even get the chance to put the leaven in their bread, and as a result of this the bread did not have time to rise. God instituted this feast so all generations would remember how the swift hand of God had moved on behalf of His people. Leaven is forbidden to be in your home during the Feast of Unleavened Bread. It is a picture of sin and therefore must be removed, every trace of it.

Removing the leaven from the home actually begins one month before the feast arrives. A tradition has emerged known as the "Bedikat Chametz," or the "Search for Leaven" ceremony.[5] One month before the Passover the mother of the home will go through the entire house and remove every trace of leaven; every bread crumb must be discovered and thrown out. She will clean every nook and cranny until she is satisfied that all of it is gone. This is possibly where we get the custom known as "Spring Cleaning."

When it is time for the feast the mother will leave out ten small pieces of leavened bread throughout the house so that the father will find them later at the ceremony.[6] The father will walk through the home with a candle, a feather, and a wooden spoon. He uses the candle as his light to find the leaven. When he finds it he uses the feather to sweep the leavened bread onto the wooden spoon. He then places the bread in a bag. After all ten pieces are found the bag is taken outside and burned so that the home is purged of all leaven.[7] This symbolic ceremony is performed to show they have kept God's commandment and have removed all sin from their home. It's important to note that you cannot celebrate the feast while there is still leaven in your home.

The central image or theme for this feast is the unleavened or "matzah" bread. During the Passover Seder meal three pieces of flat matzah bread, which look like large soda crackers, are placed in the three compartments of a linen "unity bag." The middle piece is called the Afikomen, which means "that which comes after." Later in the ceremony the Afikomen is removed and broken, then wrapped in a special cloth and hidden in the home until still later.[8]

People have wondered for centuries why the middle bread is broken and not the top or the bottom ones. Some have suggested that the three breads stand for Abraham, Isaac, and Jacob. Some say they represent the Priests, the Levites, and the Israelites. The problem with these interpretations is that neither Isaac nor the Levites were broken. So what does it mean to have the middle bread broken? We find the answer in the New Testament teaching on the Trinity. We see the Father, the Son, and the Holy Spirit. The Son's body is broken, He is then wrapped and put away in the earth and on the third day is brought back to life. So in the ceremony of the Afikomen we find a picture of the death (breaking) and burial (hiding) of the Messiah.

This matzah bread has three characteristics to it that set it apart from other types of bread and provide us with another powerful picture of Jesus. It is bruised because it is beaten into shape, it has stripes because of the way it is grilled, and finally it is pierced many times to allow for proper cooking. Isaiah 53:5 says Jesus was bruised: "He was bruised for our iniquities." The same verse also says He received stripes on His back: "And with his stripes we are healed." Zechariah 12:10 tells us that the Messiah would be pierced: "They will look on me, the one they have pierced."

Another symbolic feature about leaven is its ability to permeate dough. Leaven has a contaminating nature. It sours and ferments the dough and causes it to swell to many times its original size without changing its weight. In fact, this souring process is the first stage of decay. And here we find some more relevance in the death of Jesus.

Psalm 15 is considered to be a Messianic Psalm. King David writes "because you will not abandon me to the grave, nor will you let your Holy One see decay." Because Jesus was the perfect Lamb and sinless as the unleavened bread represents, God did not allow His body to decay in the grave. So we see Jesus as the fulfillment of the prophetic picture portrayed in the Feast of Unleavened Bread.

What is God saying to us through this feast? Is it about not eating bread with leaven? I think there is something more, profoundly more, to this feast. Just as the Scripture commanded that the Israelites remove all leaven from their homes, we, too, are called to remove all the sin from our homes, both literally and spiritually. It was impossible for them to celebrate the Passover with any leaven in their homes. We cannot come into the Kingdom of God with sin in our hearts. We need to ask the Holy Spirit to come and reveal to us any hidden leaven or sin in our hearts. May we all strive to do what the Apostle Paul told the early church to do using the illustration of the Feast of Unleavened Bread in 1 Corinthians 5:6–8: "Your boasting is not good. Don't you know that a little yeast works through the whole batch of dough? Get rid of the old yeast that you may be a new batch without yeast—as you really are. For Christ, our Passover lamb, has been sacrificed. Therefore let us keep the Festival, not with the old yeast, the yeast of malice and wickedness, but with bread without yeast, the bread of sincerity and truth."

The Resurrection—the Feast of Firstfruits

After His death, as pictured in the Passover Feast, Jesus remained in the tomb for three days, as depicted in the Feast of Unleavened Bread. Then comes the resurrection on Sunday morning, which is symbolized by the Feast of Firstfruits. Here is how Leviticus commands it be kept:

> The Lord said to Moses, "Speak to the Israelites and say to them: 'When you enter the land I am going to give you and you reap its harvest, bring to the priest a sheaf of the first grain you harvest. He is to wave the sheaf before the Lord so it will be accepted on your behalf; the priest is to wave it on the day after the Sabbath. On the day you wave the sheaf, you must sacrifice as a burnt offering to the Lord a lamb a year old without defect, together with its grain offering of two-tenths of an ephah of fine flour mixed with oil—an offering made to the Lord by fire, a pleasing aroma—and its drink offering of a quarter of a hin of wine. You must not eat any bread, or roasted or new grain, until the very day you bring this offering to your God. This is to be a lasting ordinance for the generations to come, wherever you live.'" (Lev. 23:9–14)

The Feast of Firstfruits has virtually disappeared since the days following the destruction of the Temple. This feast focuses on the idea of first things. Through this feast we see the Lord speaking to us about two powerful images. The first image is in the area of giving our tithes to the Lord. The second picture is that of the resurrection of Jesus from the dead, which serves as a guarantee of our own resurrection. Before we move into the parallels of this feast, it would be good for me to lay a foundation and go back in time and look at the original meaning and practices involved in celebrating it.

The Feast of Firstfruits is the third feast in the Jewish festive cycle. On the Hebrew calendar it occurred on the sixteenth day of Nissan, which coincides with our March or April. As stated previously, Passover took place on the fourteenth and Unleavened Bread on the fifteenth. Just as these first three feasts happened consecutively, so Jesus fulfilled them in like manner through His death, burial, and resurrection.

Like many of Israel's feasts, Firstfruits revolved around the agricultural cycle of the land. Barley was the first grain to ripen of all the grains that were sown during the winter months. For the Feast of Firstfruits, a sheaf (about a bushel) of barley would be harvested and brought to the Temple as a thanksgiving offering to the Lord for the harvest. According to Leviticus 23:11, the High Priest was to take the first fruits the person brought to the Temple and wave them before the Lord. God would see this, He would accept the offering of the first fruits, and then the people were free to enjoy the harvest. The bushel was brought in as a representation of the entire field. Their bringing in this small portion was really an act of faith showing God the people believed He would bring in a full harvest that year.

How does this apply to the Lord Jesus? In 1 Corinthians 15:20-23, Paul writes: "But Christ has indeed been raised from the dead, the firstfruits of those who have fallen asleep. For since death came through a man, the resurrection of the dead comes also through a man. For as in Adam all die, so in Christ all will be made alive. But each in his own turn: Christ, the firstfruits; then, when he comes, those who belong to him." Since the death of Jesus made full atonement for our sins, His resurrection is the final proof that God accepted His sacrifice and that we are indeed forgiven (Rom. 4:25). Just as the wave offering at the Feast of Firstfruits pointed toward and assured the people that the full harvest would be reaped, so the resurrection of Jesus points toward and provides full assurance that we, too, will rise from the dead one day. Jesus is our wave sheaf that guarantees God's promise of eternal life!

The Ascension and Giving of the Spirit—the Feast of Pentecost

Following the resurrection, Jesus appeared to numbers of believers in a variety of situations (1 Cor. 15:3–7). He also instructed the Apostles for a period of forty days concerning the Kingdom of God (Acts 1:1–3). Finally the time had come for Him to return to His Father. After instructing them to wait for the promise of the Holy Spirit, Jesus ascended into heaven from the

Mount of Olives which was to the east of Jerusalem (Acts 1:9–11).

The Apostles returned to the Upper Room in Jerusalem and began to seek the Lord in prayer for the next ten days. Since Jesus died on Passover, then stayed on earth another forty days, the Ascension occurred just ten days before the Feast of Pentecost. The momentous events of Acts 2:1–4 with the coming of the Holy Spirit on the church took place exactly on the date of this important biblical feast. Let's look at the instructions surrounding its celebration from the Old Testament:

> From the day after the Sabbath, the day you brought the sheaf of the wave offering, count off seven full weeks. Count off fifty days up to the day after the seventh Sabbath, and then present an offering of new grain to the Lord. From wherever you live, bring two loaves made of two-tenths of an ephah of fine flour, baked with yeast, as a wave offering of Firstfruits to the Lord. Present with this bread seven male lambs, each a year old and without defect, one young bull and two rams. They will be a burnt offering to the Lord, together with their grain offerings and drink offerings—an offering made by fire, an aroma pleasing to the Lord. Then sacrifice one male goat for a sin offering and two lambs, each a year old, for a fellowship offering. The priest is to wave the two lambs before the Lord as a wave offering, together with the bread of the Firstfruits. They are a sacred offering to the Lord for the priest. On that same day you are to proclaim a

> sacred assembly and do no regular work. This is to be a lasting ordinance for the generations to come, wherever you live. When you reap the harvest of your land, do not reap to the very edges of your field or gather the gleanings of your harvest. Leave them for the poor and the alien. I am the Lord your God. (Lev. 23:15–22)

We now come to one of the most widely recognized feasts in the Church—Pentecost. The first thing we should note about this feast is the fact that the Day of Pentecost mentioned in Acts 2 is not the very first occurrence of the Feast of Pentecost. Actually, according to Jewish tradition, the very first occurrence of the Day of Pentecost happened on the day God gave Moses the Torah at the foot of Mount Sinai almost thirty-five hundred years ago. Fifty days after the crossing of the Red Sea, God gives the law to be written in stone. Most believers are under the impression that the Day of Pentecost after the resurrection of Christ was the first time it had ever happened in Israel. In fact, we will discover that there was an expectation within the hearts of first-century Jews for God to pour out His Spirit on that very day.[9]

Before we proceed any further I think it would be good for us to examine some of the parallels between the Mount Sinai account of the Day of Pentecost and the New Testament account of that day. The original Feast of Pentecost takes place fifty days after the crossing of the Red Sea. That crossing was a type of Firstfruits, and just like today, Pentecost takes place on the fiftieth day after the Feast of Firstfruits. In modern-day Judaism Pentecost is celebrated as the anniversary of the giving of the Torah, or the Law, to Israel at Mount Sinai. At the first Feast of Pentecost, the Law of God is written on tablets of stone. Remember earlier how I said that the Apostle Paul told us in Colossians that the feasts were shadows of things to come (2:16, 17). So basically what that means is there are parallels between the feasts and certain events in the New Testament and also in the future.

Let's examine the events of the first Feast of Pentecost according to rabbinical tradition, and then we will compare it to the Acts version and see if we can come up with any similarities. Exodus 19 describes the giving of the Torah. This is where God spoke to the people from Mount Sinai. The power of what happened at this monumental event eludes the English reader. In Exodus 19:19, a trumpet (shofar) was sounded. The trumpet grew louder and louder. Exodus 19:19 says: "And God answered him with thunder [by a voice KJV]." Exodus 20:18 says, "And all the people perceived the thunder [saw the thunderings KJV]." So the Bible records hints at the possibility that the people who were gathered at the foot of Mount Sinai actually saw the words as they came out of the mouth of the Lord.

This is what is says in the Midrash (a rabbinic commentary on the Scriptures) in Rabbah 5:9: "When God gave the Torah on Sinai He displayed untold marvels to Israel with His voice. What happened? God spoke and the voice reverberated throughout the whole world. It says, and all the people witnessed the thunderings."

It's important for us to note that it says "the thunderings" and not "the thunder." There was a world-famous rabbi by the name of Rabbi Yohanan ben Zakkai, and in this same Midrash he says that "God's voice, as it was uttered, split up into seventy voices, in seventy languages, so that all the nations should understand." That's awesome to try to comprehend. So God was not speaking to one particular race or people; the guidelines of the Torah were for all people for all time.

Now read what Rabbi Moshe Weissman wrote in the Midrash about the first Feast of Pentecost:

> In the occasion of the giving of the Torah, the children of Israel not only heard the Lord's voice but actually saw the sound waves as they emerged from the Lord's mouth. They visualized them as a fiery substance. Each commandment that left the Lord's mouth traveled around the entire Camp and then to each Jew individually, asking him, "Do you accept upon yourself this Commandment with all the Jewish law pertaining to it?" Every Jew answered, "Yes" after each commandment. Finally, the fiery substance which they saw engraved itself on the tablets.

Wind, fire, and different languages being spoken—does that sound familiar to anyone?

Let's look at its counterpart as found in Acts 2:1–11:

> When the day of Pentecost came, they were all to-

gether in one place. Suddenly a sound like the blowing of a violent wind came from heaven and filled the whole house where they were sitting. They saw what seemed to be tongues of fire that separated and came to rest on each of them. All of them were filled with the Holy Spirit and began to speak in other tongues as the Spirit enabled them.

Now there were staying in Jerusalem God-fearing Jews from every nation under heaven. When they heard this sound, a crowd came together in bewilderment, because each one heard them speaking in his own language. Utterly amazed, they asked: "Are not all these men who are speaking Galileans? Then how is it that each of us hears them in his own native language? Parthians, Medes and Elamites; residents of Mesopotamia, Judea and Cappadocia, Pontus and Asia, Phrygia and Pamphylia, Egypt and the parts of Libya near Cyrene; visitors from Rome (both Jews and converts to Judaism); Cretans and Arabs—we hear them declaring the wonders of God in our own tongues!"

I want to paint a picture for you as we examine the events of the Day of Pentecost. We need to ask ourselves some basic questions surrounding the details of this event: How was it that there just happened to be all these thousands of men at the Temple that day? Was that the normal amount of activity for any given day, or was there something special happening that day?

The Bible declares that there are three pilgrim feasts

that all men must attend. They are Passover, Pentecost, and Tabernacles (Deut. 16:16). What that means is all males had to go to Jerusalem for these required Feasts of the Lord. The implication is that making the journey to Jerusalem for the other feasts was optional but for these three was mandatory. Therefore, we can deduce that at this particular Feast of Pentecost, being one of the pilgrim feasts, a large number of the males living in and around Israel were probably at the Temple on that day to celebrate the Feast of Pentecost.

The text says that the day of Pentecost was "fully come." What does that mean? God told the people that they were to count seven weeks from the Feast of Firstfruits and then on the fiftieth day they were to celebrate Pentecost. This was known as the "Counting of the Omer." So the feast had "fully come" on the fiftieth day. This explains why all those men were at the Temple.

They are in the Temple and they are worshiping the Lord. They are thanking God for giving them the Torah. The Feast of Pentecost is the celebration of the giving of the Law. The people were expecting God to do something they had read about for generations.

During the Temple service for Pentecost they would have heard the Scriptures read. This included Jeremiah 31:31–33:

> "The time is coming," declares the Lord, "when I will make a new covenant with the house of Israel and with the house of Judah. It will not be like the covenant I made with their forefathers when I took them by the hand to lead them out of Egypt, because they broke my

> covenant, though I was a husband to them," declares the Lord. "This is the covenant I will make with the house of Israel after that time," declares the Lord. "I will put my law in their minds and write it on their hearts. I will be their God, and they will be my people."

The prophet promises that one day God will write His law in the hearts of His people by His Spirit. He no longer wanted a people who just knew the law with their minds. He did not want the law to be written in stone any longer, but rather He wanted it to be written in their hearts. They would also have read from the Book of Joel—that's why Peter quotes from it when he addresses the crowd. They were reminded of how God spoke to them through thunder and fire and all kinds of marvelous signs. Imagine what must have been happening in the minds of these men as they were leaving the Temple area.

As they leave, they hear the sound of a mighty rushing wind. As they are descending the Temple Mount, they see people starting to gather at the Upper Room. Something is going on. When they arrive they hear the voices speaking in all different kinds of languages, they remember: the fire, the wind, the voices in many languages. This is what they were taught happened at Sinai centuries before on that very day, the Feast of Pentecost. Is there any wonder three thousand of them accepted Christ that day? In their minds, there was no room for interpretation or error. The words of the prophets were coming to pass right before their eyes and they knew it.

Contrast this with what happened after the first Pentecost. God birthed the nation of Israel at the foot of Mount Sinai, where His presence was made manifest to them that day. After such a glorious revelation of God and the historic event of the giving of the Torah, what did Israel do? They couldn't wait for God. Even though the memory of what God had just done in the Exodus and the momentous event of the giving of the Law was still fresh in their minds, they turned their hearts away from God and made themselves a golden calf to worship.

The response that Aaron gave to Moses is classic. Moses left Aaron in charge while he went up to the mountain to receive the Law. When he leaves they are a people who are filled with excitement and anticipation of what God is going to do next. By the time he comes back down they are worshiping a golden calf. What happened? Aaron says, "We threw in the gold and out came a cow." God's response to this idolatry results in death. So on the first day of Pentecost three thousand people are killed, as Exodus 32:28 records: "The Levites did as Moses commanded, and that day about three thousand of the people died."

Look at the contrast that we find in Acts 2:41: "Those who accepted his message were baptized, and about three thousand were added to their number that day." On the Day of Pentecost that Jesus fulfilled, three thousand are saved. The giving of the Law brings death because of the people's sin. The coming of the Spirit brings life, eternal life, because of the grace of God available through the gospel.

Conclusion

Our exploration of first-century Jewish culture and the ways in which it enhances our understanding of the words and deeds of Jesus has been based upon the premise that the roots of the church of Jesus Christ are Jewish. As Paul writes in Romans 11:16b–18, "If the root is holy, so are the branches. If some of the branches have been broken off, and you, though a wild olive shoot, have been grafted in among the others and now share in the nourishing sap from the olive root, do not boast over those branches. If you do, consider this: You do not support the root, but the root supports you."

He is referring to the biblical picture of Israel as God's olive tree (Jer. 11:16). The original root of the people of God is Israel, those whom He chose out of all the tribes of the earth to know Him and to make Him known (Deut. 7:6). Those of us who are Gentiles have, by the grace of God, been grafted into the people of God. We cannot cut ourselves off from our spiritual roots and expect to survive, let alone flourish. Thus the church cannot afford to ignore her Hebraic roots.

I pray that this book has stirred you to learn more about our Jewish roots as the people of God as we follow after the One our Hebrew Christian brothers and sisters call Yeshua Ha Mashiach, Jesus the Messiah!

Endnotes

Introduction

1. See, for example, Craig L. Blomberg, *Jesus and the Gospels* (Nashville: Broadman and Holman, 1997); Merrill C. Tenney, *New Testament Survey*, rev. ed. (Grand Rapids, MI: Wm. B. Eerdmans, 1985); and Robert H. Gundry, *A Survey of the New Testament*, rev. ed. (Grand Rapids, MI: Zondervan, 1981).
2. See the Canons of the Council of Laodicea, Canon XXIX.
3. Robin Sampson and Linda Pierce, *The Family Guide to Biblical Holidays with Activities for All Ages* (Woodbridge, VA: Heart of Mission Publishing, 2001), p. 40.

Chapter 1 – Jesus and John

1. Mishnah, Ta'anit 4:2.
2. Brad H. Young, *Jesus the Jewish Theologian* (Peabody, MA: Hendrickson Publishers, 1995), p. 19.

Chapter 2 – The Ministry in Galilee

1. The Bible uses a term for leprosy that stood for a number of skin diseases that probably included what medical science calls leprosy today.
2. Rabbi Jack Farber, "What Is Messianic Judaism?" http://www.cmy.on.ca/Messianic_Judaism/messianic.htm.
3. Ron Moseley, *Yeshua: A Guide to the Real Jesus and the Original Church* (Baltimore: Lederer Books, 1996), p. 21.
4. Ibid.
5. Ibid., p. 22.
6. David Bivin and Ron Blizzard, Jr., *Understanding the Difficult Words of Jesus*, rev. ed. (Dayton: Center for Judaic-Christian Studies, 1994), p. 114.
7. Mosley, *Yeshua*, p. 22; Bivin and Blizzard, *Understanding the Difficult Words of Jesus*, pp. 105–106.

Chapter 3 – At the Feast in Jerusalem

1. Robin Sampson and Linda Pierce, *The Family Guide to Biblical Holidays with Activities for All Ages* (Wood-

bridge, VA: Heart of Mission Publishing, 2001), p. 281.

2. Ibid., pp. 283, 284.
3. Ibid., p. 282.
4. Edward Chumney, *The Seven Festivals of the Messiah* (Shippensburg, PA: Treasure House, 1994), p .111.
5. Talmud, Rosh haShannah 16b.
6. Sampson and Pierce, *Family Guide*, p. 289.
7. Talmud, Rosh haShannah 16b.
8. Chumney, *Seven Festivals*, pp. 118, 119.
9. Ibid., pp. 120–122.
10. Ibid., p. 121.
11. Ibid., p. 123.
12. Ibid., p. 124.
13. Ibid.
14. Sampson and Pierce, *Family Guide*, p. 286.
15. Chumney, *Seven Festivals*, p. 112.
16. Ibid., pp. 127, 128; Talmud, Rosh haShannah 16b.
17. Sampson and Pierce, *Family Guide*, p. 319.
18. Ibid., p. 321.
19. Alfred Edersheim, *The Temple, Its Ministry and Services* (1874; repr. Peabody, MA: Hendrickson Publishers, 1994), p. 258; Chumney, *Seven Festivals*, p. 135.
20. Chumney, *Seven Festivals*, p. 136.
21. Talmud, Yoma 4:2.
22. Talmud, Yoma 39b.
23. Edersheim, *Temple*, pp. 226–227; Mishnah, Succah 5; Talmud, Sukkah 51a–b; Chumney, *Seven Festivals*, p. 169.
24. Edersheim, *Temple*, pp. 220–223; Chumney, *Seven Festivals*, pp. 171–172.

25. Edersheim, *Temple*, pp. 224–226; Chumney, *Seven Festivals*, p. 175; Mishnah, Sukkah 5:2–3.

Chapter 4 – The Ministry in Judea

1. Josephus, *Antiquities* 12:324–325.
2. Jerusalem Talmud, Moed Katan 1:5.
3. Ibid.
4. Ron Mosely, *Yeshua: A Guide to the Real Jesus and the Original Church* (Baltimore: Lederer Books, 1996), p. 27.
5. John F. Walvoord and Roy B. Zuck, *The Bible Knowledge Commentary,* New Testament ed. (n.p.: Victor Books, 1983), s.v. Matthew 19:23–26.
6. George M. Lamsa, *Idioms of the Bible Explained and a Key to the Original Gospels* (San Francisco: HarperSanFrancisco, 1995), p. 54.
7. "Bar Kappara taught: Until three days [after death] the soul keeps on returning to the grave, thinking that it will go back [into the body]; but when it sees that the facial features have become disfigured, it departs and abandons it [the body]" (Mishnah, Genesis Rabbah 100:7).

Chapter 5 – The Final Week in Jerusalem

1. Mishnah, Shekalim 7:4.
2. Craig S. Keener, *The IVP Bible Background Commentary: New Testament* (Downers Grove, IL: InterVarsity

Press, 1993), s.v. Matthew 21:1–11.

3. Robin Sampson and Linda Pierce, *The Family Guide to Biblical Holidays with Activities for All Ages* (Woodbridge, VA: Heart of Mission Publishing, 2001), p. 128; Edward Chumney, *The Seven Festivals of the Messiah* (Shippensburg, PA: Treasure House, 1994), p. 26.
4. Josephus, *Jewish War* 2:167–177, *Antiquities* 18:55–62.
5. Sampson and Pierce, *Family Guide*, p. 111.
6. Mishnah, Shekalim 7:4.
7. Sampson and Pierce, *Family Guide*, p. 127.
8. Alfred Edersheim, *The Temple, Its Ministry and Services* (1874; repr. Peabody, MA: Hendrickson Publishers, 1994), p. 177.

Chapter 6 – Crucifixion to Pentecost

1. Edward Chumney, *The Seven Festivals of the Messiah* (Shippensburg, PA: Treasure House, 1994), p. 29; Alfred Edersheim, *The Temple, Its Ministry and Services* (1874; repr. Peabody, MA: Hendrickson Publishers, 1994), p. 174.
2. A piece of the Temple wall was found near the Temple Mount with an inscription, "Place of trumpeting" in Hebrew. Asher S. Kaufman, "Where Was the Trumpeting Inscription Located," "Queries & Comments," *Biblical Archaeology Review* 13:03.
3. Chumney, *Seven Festivals*, p. 46.
4. Code of Jewish Law, Yoreh Deah 340:1, 374:4; Mishnah, Moed Katan 3:5.

5. Robin Sampson and Linda Pierce, *The Family Guide to Biblical Holidays with Activities for All Ages* (Woodbridge, VA: Heart of Mission Publishing, 2001), p. 167; Chumney, *Seven Festivals*, p. 50.
6. Chumney, *Seven Festivals*, p. 51.
7. Sampson and Pierce, *Family Guide*, pp. 171–172.
8. Malka Drucker, *Passover: A Season of Freedom* (New York: Holiday House, 1981), p. 51.
9. Edersheim, *Temple*, p. 206; Chumney, *Seven Festivals*, pp. 71, 72; Sampson and Pierce, *Family Guide*, p. 229.

Bibliography

Aland, Kurt, ed. *Synopsis of the Four Gospels.* 2nd ed. n.p.: United Bible Societies, 1975.

Avi-Yonah, Michael, ed. *A History of Israel and the Holy Land.* New York: Steinmatsky, 2001.

Bivin, David, and Ron Blizzard, Jr. *Understanding the Difficult Words of Jesus.* Rev. ed. Dayton: Center for Judaic-Christian Studies, 1994.

Blomberg, Craig L. *Interpreting the Parables.* Downers Grove, IL: InterVarsity Press, 1990.

———. *Jesus and the Gospels.* Nashville: Broadman and Holman, 1997.

Booker, Richard. *Jesus in the Feasts of Israel.* South Plainfield, NJ: Bridge Publishing, 1987.

Brickner, David. *Christ in the Feast of Tabernacles.* Chicago: Moody Press, 2006.

Bruce, F. F. *Paul, Apostle of the Heart Set Free.* Grand Rapids, MI: William B. Eerdmans, 1977.

Cairns, Earl. *Christianity through the Centuries.* Grand Rapids, MI: Academie Books, 1981.

Chumney, Edward. *The Seven Festivals of the Messiah*. Shippensburg, PA: Treasure House, 1994.

Cohen, Abraham. *Everyman's Talmud*. New York: Schocken Books, 1949.

Cohen, Moishe. *Messianic Messages Out of Zion*. Tupelo, MS: Messianic Messages, 2002.

Crossan, John Dominic. *Jesus: A Revolutionary Biography*. San Francisco: HarperSanFrancisco, 1994.

Dershowitz, Alan. *The Case for Israel*. Hoboken, NJ: John Wiley & Sons, 2003.

Drucker, Malka. *Passover: A Season of Freedom*. New York: Holiday House, 1981.

Edersheim, Alfred. *The Life and Times of Jesus the Messiah*. Peabody, MA: Hendrickson Publishers, 1993.

———. *The Temple, Its Ministry and Services*. 1874. Reprint. Peabody, MA: Hendrickson Publishers, 1994.

Epp, Theodore. *Portraits of Christ in the Tabernacle*. Lincoln, NE: Back to the Bible, 1976.

Eusebius of Caesarea. *The History of the Church*. Translated by G. A. Williamson. London: Penguin Books, 1989.

Evans, Craig. *Fabricating Jesus, How Modern Scholars Distort the Gospels*. Downers Grove, IL: IVP Books, 2006.

———. *Jesus and the Ossuaries: What Jewish Burial Practices Reveal about the Beginning of Christianity*. Waco, TX: Baylor University Press, 2003.

Flusser, David. *Jewish Sources in Early Christianity*.

Translated by John Glucker. Tel Aviv: MOD Books, 1989.

———. *Judaism and the Origins of Christianity.* Jerusalem: Magnes Press, 1988.

Fruchtenbaum, Arnold G. *The Footsteps of the Messiah*. Rev. ed. Tustin, CA: Ariel Ministries, 2004.

———. *Israelology: The Missing Link in Systematic Theology.* Tustin, CA: Ariel Ministries, 2001.

Gundry, Robert H. *A Survey of the New Testament.* Rev. ed. Grand Rapids, MI: Zondervan, 1981.

Heim, Ralph Daniel. *A Harmony of the Gospels.* Philadelphia: Fortress, 1947.

Jeremias, Joachim. *Jerusalem in the Time of Jesus.* Philadelphia: Fortress, 1969.

Josephus, Flavius. *The Complete Works of Josephus.* Translated by William Whiston. Grand Rapids, MI: Kregel Publications, 1999.

Kasdan, Barney. *God's Appointed Times: A Practical Guide for Understanding and Celebrating the Biblical Holidays*. Baltimore: Lederer Books, 1993.

Keener, Craig S. *The IVP Bible Background Commentary: New Testament*. Downers Grove, IL: InterVarsity Press, 1993.

Lachs, Samuel Tobias. *A Rabbinic Commentary on the New Testament*. Hoboken, NJ: Ktav Publishing House, 1987.

Lamsa, George M. *Idioms of the Bible Explained and a Key to the Original Gospels*. San Francisco: HarperSanFrancisco, 1995.

Lancaster, D. Thomas. *Restoration: Returning the To-*

rah of God to the Disciples of Jesus. Littleton, CO: First Fruits of Zion, 2005.

Levine, Amy-Jill. *The Misunderstood Jew: The Church and the Scandal of the Jewish Jesus*. New York: HarperOne, 2006.

Levine, Amy-Jill, Dale C. Allison Jr., and John Dominic Crossan, eds. *The Historical Jesus in Context*. Princeton, NJ: Princeton University Press, 2006.

Luther, Martin. *The Jews and Their Lies*. 1543. Reprint. York, SC: Liberty Bell Publications, 2004.

Moseley, Ron. *Yeshua: A Guide to the Real Jesus and the Original Church*. Baltimore: Lederer Books, 1996.

Resnik, Russell L. *The Root and the Branches, Jewish Identity in Messiah*. Albuquerque, NM: Adat Yeshua, 1997.

Reuven, Zaide. *Tabernacles—Succoth: When the Messiah Feasts with Jews and Gentiles*. Dallas: Zaide Reuven Ezrog Farm, 1999.

Rosen, Ceil and Moishe. *Christ in the Passover.* Chicago: Moody Press, 2006.

Sampson, Robin, and Linda Pierce. *The Family Guide to Biblical Holidays with Activities for All Ages*. Woodbridge, VA: Heart of Mission Publishing, 2001.

Schmalz, Reuven Efraim, and Raymond Robert Fischer. *The Messianic Seal of the Jerusalem Church*. Tiberias: Olim Publications, 1999.

Stern, David H., trans. *The Complete Bible*. Clarksville, MD: Jewish New Testament Publications, 1998.

———. *Jewish New Testament Commentary.* Clarksville, MD: Jewish New Testament Publications, 1992.

———. *Restoring the Jewishness of the Gospel: A Message for Christians.* Jerusalem: Jewish New Testament Publications, 1988.

Stern, Sam. *The Victory of Light.* Pensacola, FL: Bible Baptist Bookstore, 1998.

Strobel, Lee. *The Case for the Real Christ.* Grand Rapids, MI: Zondervan, 2007.

Tenney, Merrill C. *New Testament Survey.* Rev. ed. Grand Rapids, MI: Wm. B. Eerdmans, 1985.

Teplinsky, Sandra. *Why Care About Israel?* Grand Rapids, MI: Chosen, 2004.

Troy, Gil. *Why I Am a Zionist: Israel, Jewish Identity and the Challenges of Today.* Montreal: Bromfman Jewish Education Centre, 2002.

Walvoord, John F., and Roy B. Zuck. *The Bible Knowledge Commentary,* New Testament ed. N.p.: Victor Books, 1983.

Wilson, Barrie. *How Jesus Became Christian.* N.p.: Random House Canada, 2008.

Young, Brad H. *Jesus the Jewish Theologian.* Peabody, MA: Hendrickson Publishers, 1995.

———. *The Parables: Jewish Tradition and Christian Interpretation.* Peabody, MA: Hendrickson Publishers, 1998.

———. *Paul the Jewish Theologian.* Peabody, MA: Hendrickson Publishers, 1997.